German
Home Cooking

More than a 100 authentic German family recipes;
passed down from generation to generation

By: Dr. Duane R. Lund

German
Home Cooking

First Printing 2008

Second Printing July 2008

Third Printing February 2010

Fourth Printing September 2012

Fifth Printing November 2014

Printed in the United States of America
by
Lund S&R Publications
Staples, Minnesota 56479

ISBN-13: 978-0-9740821-5-8
ISBN-10: 0-9740821-5-5

Dedication

To the many thousands of German families who migrated to the
United States and Canada and who brought with them so many
fabulous recipes for their wonderful German cuisine.

With Appreciation

To Dr. Greg and Joyce Pappenfus who helped so much in collecting these recipes.

Table of Contents

Chapter I ~ Soups and Stews

Chapter II ~ Dumplings and Potato Pancakes

Chapter III ~ Bread

Chapter IV ~ Salads

Chapter V ~ Meats

Fish

Chapter VI ~ Vegetables

Table of Contents continued

Chapter VII ~ Casseroles

Chapter VIII ~ Desserts

Chapter IX ~ Home Brew

Soups and Stews

Chapter One

Beer Cheese Soup * (*Biersuppe mit käse*)

Ingredients to serve 4:

1/4 pound (1 stick) butter or margarine or 8 T oil
1/2 t seasoned salt
1/4 t celery salt
1 t Worcestershire sauce
1/2 cup diced onion
1/4 cup diced celery
1/2 cup flour
2 cns. condensed chicken broth
1 cn. (12 oz.) beer
2 cups shredded cheddar cheese
popcorn for garnish (optional)

Melt butter in a large saucepan; add seasonings; onions and celery. Cook over medium heat until vegetables are softened. Add flour, whisking to blend. Cook until bubbly; reduce heat to low and add remaining ingredients, whisking until cheese melts.

Garnish with popcorn (optional)

*Courtesy (the late) Max Ruttger III, Gull Lake, Minnesota

Beer Soup with Egg Noodles *(Biersuppe mit Nudeln)*

Ingredients to serve 4-6:

3 cups cooked egg noodles
1/4 pound butter or margarine (1stick) cut into half-inch chunks
2 T cinnamon
Salt and pepper to taste
3 cns. beer of your choosing (not refrigerated)
Crouton-size pieces of dark rye bread for garnish

As soon as the cooked egg noodles have been drained, stir in the butter slices until they melt. Stir in the pepper, salt and cinnamon. Cover the noodles with the beer. Heat until hot but do not let boil.

Garnish with bits of rye bread.

Ingredients to serve 4:

1/8 pound butter or margarine (1/2 stick) or 4 T oil
1 onion, peeled and chopped
2 medium carrots, scraped and chopped
2 celery ribs, chopped
2 medium potatoes, peeled and diced
1 green bell pepper, seeded and chopped
2 cups chicken broth
4 T flour
1-1/2 cups water
4 oz. cheddar cheese, grated or diced small
1/2 t cumin
1/2 t thyme
1 t pepper
chopped celery leaves for garnish

Sauté onions, celery, pepper and carrots 2 or 3 minutes until onion is translucent. Move to a soup pot. Add all ingredients. Sprinkle in flour and continue to heat and stir another 2 or 3 minutes.

Carrot Soup with Apple *(Möhrensuppe mit Äpfeln)*

Ingredients to serve 6:

8 carrots, sliced thin
2 hard apples, peeled, cored and chopped
1 onion, peeled and chopped
1 clove garlic, minced
2 ribs celery, chopped
5 cups chicken broth
1/8 pound butter (1/2 stick)
2 bay leaves
1/8 t black pepper
parsley, in sprigs or chopped for garnish

Sauté the carrots, apples, celery, onion and garlic in the butter (about 3 minutes or until the onion is translucent). Transfer to a soup kettle. Add all other ingredients and bring to a boil. Reduce heat to simmer and cook 30 minutes or until carrots are tender. Let cool. Remove bay leaves. Purée in batches. Return to kettle and cook until piping hot.

Garnish with parsley.

Soups and Stews

Creamy Cauliflower* (Blumenkohlsuppe)

Ingredients to serve 6-8:

1-1/2 pounds trimmed cauliflower, rinsed and diced
3 cups chicken broth
2 cups water plus enough water to cover cauliflower to start
1 cup cream
1 t curry powder (less if you don't like spicy food)
sprigs of parsley to garnish

Cover diced cauliflower with water. Bring to a boil; remove from heat and let stand 2 minutes. Drain and rinse with cold water. Return cauliflower to kettle; add chicken broth, 3 cups water and curry powder. Bring to a boil, then reduce heat to simmer and cook for 15 minutes. Let cool enough to handle.
Purée in batches. Return to kettle. Stir in cream. Re-heat, thoroughly, but do not let boil. Garnish with sprigs of parsley.

*Broccoli may be substituted for cauliflower.

Use either saltwater or freshwater fish.

Ingredients to serve 6:

2 pounds smoked fish (remove bones) cut bite-size.
4 potatoes, peeled and cut into bite-size chunks
2 medium onions, peeled and chopped
salt to taste (other seasonings may be added, such as white pepper, thyme, dill
or your favorite)
2 T parsley, chopped
4 T butter, margarine or oil
3 cups cream
parsley, chopped, for garnish

Cover the potato chunks with water and boil until done. Meanwhile, sauté the onion in the butter. Using the pan in which you sautéed the onion, add the potatoes, cream and seasonings. Simmer (do not boil) until all ingredients are hot. Serve in shallow bowls over pieces of smoked fish and garnish with the chopped parsley.

Hamburger and Vegetable Soup

(Haekfleisch und Gemüsesuppe)

Ingredients to serve 10:

1/8 pound butter or margarine (1/2 stick) melted, or 4 T oil
1 medium onion, chopped fine
2 ribs celery, chopped fine
2 cloves garlic, minced
1-1/2 pounds ground beef
1/2 cup cracker or bread crumbs
2 t minced parsley
1 t oregano
1 t chili powder
2 potatoes, peeled and diced
3 carrots, sliced thin
2 parsnips, scraped and chopped
1 small rutabaga, diced
2 cns. tomatoes, Italian style
6 cups beef broth
1 t thyme
1 t cumin

Garnish with parsley sprigs

Ruttger's Lentil Soup[*]

Ingredients to serve 10:
2 cups lentil beans, rinsed
2 t salt
4 cups water

Place in a covered saucepan, simmer over low heat until tender (1-1/2 hours).
Water will be mostly absorbed by the beans.

2 T butter or margarine or oil
2 t seasoned salt
2 carrots, minced
2 ribs celery, minced
2 medium potatoes, peeled and diced
1 medium onion, peeled and diced

Melt butter over medium heat. Add salt. Add vegetables and sauté, tossing and stirring
occasionally until softened. Add 8 cups water (if desired, 1 cup of liquid can be dry white wine
or sherry). Add lentils, simmer 1 hour, stirring occasionally.

*Courtesy (the late) Max Ruttger III, Gull Lake, Minnesota

Ingredients to serve 8:

1-1/2 cups green lentils, rinsed
1/8 pound butter or margarine (1/2 stick)
1 onion (large), peeled and chopped
3 ribs celery, chopped
1 carrot (large), sliced thin
3 leeks, white parts only, chopped
3 cloves garlic, minced
6 cups water
salt and pepper to taste
3 T chives, chopped, for garnish

In the melted butter, sauté onions, carrots, garlic and celery a few minutes until onion is translucent. Transfer to a soup pot. Add all other ingredients except chives. Simmer about 1 hour or until lentils are tender. Spoon into bowls and garnish with chopped chives.

Onion and Garlic Soup *(Zwiebelsuppe mit Knoblauch)*

Ingredients to serve 8:

6 medium onions, peeled and sliced
6 heads garlic, peeled and cut into quarters
1 cup water
6 cups beef broth
1/2 cup white wine
1/2 t thyme
salt and pepper to taste
1/4 pound grated cheese of your choosing for garnish

Place garlic and onion pieces in a small baking dish. Cover with 1 cup of water and 1/2 cup wine. Bake 1 hour at 325˚.

Remove from oven and place onion, liquid and garlic in a soup pot. Separate onion rings and garlic cloves with a fork. Add beef broth and spices. Bring to a boil, then reduce to simmer for 1 hour.

Serve hot with grated cheese on surface.

Split Pea Soup with Potatoes
(Erbensuppe mit Kartoffeln)

Ingredients to serve 8:

1/8 pound butter or margarine, melted (1/2 stick) or 4 T oil
1 onion, peeled and chopped
2 ribs celery, chopped
2 carrots, chopped
1 pound dry split peas, rinsed
3/4 pound ham, cubed bite-size
7 cups water
2 chicken bouillon cubes
2 medium potatoes, peeled and cubed
1 t tarragon
1 t poultry seasoning
salt and pepper to taste
croutons for garnish

Sauté the onion and celery in the melted butter a few minutes until onion is translucent. Combine all ingredients in a soup pot and simmer 1-1/2 hours (or longer if vegetables are not tender).

Garnish with croutons.

Puréed Fresh Green Pea Soup *(Erbensuppe)*

Ingredients to serve 4-6:

5 slices bacon, fried crisp and broken into bits (for garnish)
1/8 pound butter or margarine, melted (1/2 stick) or 4 T oil
1 medium onion, chopped fine
4 cups shelled fresh (or frozen) peas
1 rib celery, chopped
3 cups chicken broth
1 t tarragon
Salt and pepper to taste

Fry or broil bacon until crisp and break into bits.
In the melted butter, sauté the onion and celery a few minutes until onion is translucent. Place all ingredients except bacon in a soup pot and simmer 5 or 6 minutes until peas are tender.

Purée soup (in batches if necessary) until smooth. Pour through a coarse sieve. Return to kettle and, using medium heat, cook until hot.

Garnish bowls with bacon bits.

Ingredients to serve 6:

3 medium potatoes, peeled and cubed
3 medium beets, diced
1 medium onion, chopped
1 rib celery, chopped
3 cups chicken broth
1 cup half and half
2 T flour
2 T oil
1 T dried, crushed spices of your choosing. You might try basil, tarragon and/or rosemary. Total spices: 1 T
Garnish with chopped chives.

Sauté the onion and celery in oil until onion pieces are clear (2 or 3 minutes). Stir in flour.
Combine onion and celery in a soup pot with the potatoes, beets, chicken broth and spices.
Bring to a boil, then reduce heat to simmer and cook covered for about 20 minutes or until potatoes are tender. Let cool until it can be safely handled.
Process or blend the mixture in batches until smooth.
Return to the kettle; add the cream. Re-heat but do not boil.

Garnish with chopped chives.

Ingredients to serve 8:

5 medium baked potatoes (skin may be left on) diced
1 medium onion, chopped
2 ribs celery, chopped
1 clove garlic, minced
1 cn. cream of chicken soup
1 cn. cream of celery soup
2 cns. water
1 cup cream
1/8 pound butter or margarine (1/2 stick) or 4 T oil
6 slices bacon, fried or broiled crisp and broken into bits
1/4 pound cheddar cheese, shredded or grated
salt and pepper to taste

Bake potatoes, let cool, cut into small chunks
Sauté the onion, celery and garlic in the melted butter a few minutes or until onion is translucent. Combine all ingredients (except bacon and cheese) in a soup pot. Simmer over low heat for 20 minutes; do not boil. Meanwhile, fry or broil bacon and break into bits. Serve soup piping hot with cheese and bacon on surface as garnish.

Ingredients to serve 6-8:

5 medium potatoes, peeled and diced
3 cns. Italian style tomatoes
1 onion, chopped
2 ribs celery, chopped
2 cloves garlic, minced
2 bay leaves
1/2 cup cream
1/2 t sage
1/2 t oregano
1/8 pound butter or margarine (1/2 stick) or 4 T oil
2 T catsup
Enough water to cover potatoes plus 4 cups
parsley or celery leaves for garnish

In the melted butter, sauté onion, celery and garlic a few minutes until onion is translucent. In a soup pot, cover the chopped potatoes with water and cook (boil) until potatoes are soft. Discard water. Add all other ingredients (including 4 cups of water and liquid in cns. of tomatoes) and bring to a boil. Reduce heat immediately and let simmer about 10 minutes. Remove bay leaves.

Garnish with parsley or celery leaves. Serve piping hot.

Potato Soup with Carrots and a hint of Orange
(Kartoffelsuppe mit Karotten)

Ingredients to serve 6:

2 large potatoes, peeled and diced
4 carrots, sliced thin
2 cns. chicken broth
2 cns. water
1 orange (juice of and rind grated)
1 bay leaf
1 T brown sugar
1 cup cream
1 t Tabasco sauce
salt and pepper

In a soup pot, combine the diced potatoes, sliced carrots, chicken broth, water, sugar, Tabasco and bay leaf. Bring to a boil, then reduce heat to simmer and cook for 20 to 30 minutes or until vegetables are tender. Let cool to handle safely. Remove and discard bay leaf. Add the grated orange rind and juice. Purée the soup in batches; return to kettle. Add cream and re-heat until piping hot but do not let boil. Season to taste.

Potato Soup with Bacon or Ham

(Kartoffelsuppe mit Speck oder Schinken)

Ingredients to serve 8:

5 large potatoes, peeled and diced
6 pieces bacon*
6 cups chicken broth or stock
2 onions, peeled and chopped
4 T butter, margarine or oil
3 leeks, sliced, including green parts
1 bay leaf
1 cup cream
1/2 cup white wine
1 t coriander
salt and pepper to taste

Sauté the onion and leeks in the butter a few minutes until translucent. Place in a soup pot with all ingredients except the cream and wine. Bring to a boil, then reduce heat to simmer and cook for 30 minutes or until the potatoes are soft. Let cool for safe handling.
Remove bay leaf.
Meanwhile, broil or fry the bacon until crisp. Break into small pieces and set aside. Purée the soup. Return to the kettle and re-heat. Serve with crumbled bacon for garnish.
*Chunks of ham may be substituted.

Duck Soup *(Entesuppe)*

Cut up in pieces 1 duck and boil with 1 onion, 2 carrots, 4 ribs of celery, allspice, a bay leaf, 1 t marjoram for 1 hour. Then add 1 cup raisins, 30 prunes, 1 apple cut up in pieces. When fruits and meat and vegetables are done, mix 1/2 cup duck blood with 2 T flour and 2 T vinegar. Add to the soup and let cook slowly 1/2 hour. The blood should be diluted with vinegar to keep it from setting. Serve with potato dumplings boiled separately.

Potato Dumplings

Grate 4 or 5 large potatoes, pour off the accumulated water and add 1/2 cup flour, a pinch of baking powder, and a T salt and boil in salted water. (Drop 1/2 T dough at a time into the boiling water to form dumplings.) Drain in cold water and serve separately. Don't add them to the boiling soup, just in your soup dish.

Fish Soup *(Fischsuppe)*

Use as many different kinds of fresh fish as are available. Wash and clean fish. Remove skin and bones. Place fish in large kettle. Cover with water, salt and pepper to taste. Add 1 onion, 2 bay leaves, about 6 peppercorns or whole allspice. Celery and carrots also can be used for flavor. Bring to a boil. Add 1/2 cup of cold water, do this 3 times as it keeps the fish firm. Then cook slowly for an hour or so. Either drain or carefully remove fish from broth. To about 1/2 cup of sour cream add a small amount of the hot broth into the sour cream slowly. When broth and cream are blended put back on fire to heat. Add more pepper for flavor. To serve, pour soup over small boiled potatoes.

Cabbage with Pork *(Kohl mit Schwein)*

Ingredients to serve 6-8:

1 medium head cabbage - diced bite-size (about 2 pounds)
1 pound cooked pork roast, diced bite-size (if not cooked, brown pieces first)
3 medium potatoes, diced
3 carrots, scraped and diced (thick slices)
6 cups chicken broth (may use water)
12 allspice (whole)
10 peppercorns
1 bay leaf
salt to taste
4 T parsley, flakes or chopped, for garnish

Place all ingredients except parsley in boiling water. Reduce heat to simmer until meat is tender (about 1 hour if meat is tender to start with). Remove bay leaf before serving.

Garnish with parsley.

Cabbage with other Vegetables *(Kohl mit Gemüse)*

Ingredients to serve 8:

1 medium head cabbage, shredded
1/8 pound butter or margarine (1/2 stick) melted or 4 T oil
3 medium onions, peeled, sliced and broken into rings
3 cups beef broth
3 cups water
3 carrots, sliced thin
2 potatoes, peeled and diced
3 ribs celery, chopped
3 tomatoes, diced
1 t pepper
salt to taste
sour cream to top each bowl of soup

Sauté onions, carrots and celery. Transfer to soup pot. Add all other ingredients except cabbage, tomatoes and sour cream. Bring to a boil then reduce heat to simmer; cook for 20 minutes. Add cabbage and continue to simmer another 10 minutes. Add tomatoes and continue to cook 10 minutes or until all vegetables are tender.

Serve with a dollop of sour cream on the surface of each bowl.

Ingredients to serve 8:

1 small chicken (stewing chicken will do)
1 head cabbage (small to medium) shredded
2 qts. water
1 large onion, sliced and broken into rings
3 T flour
2 t salt
10 whole peppercorns
3 bay leaves
chopped parsley for garnish

In a large soup pot, cover the whole chicken with the water and add the cabbage, onion, salt, peppercorns and bay leaves. Bring to a boil, then reduce to simmer and cook, covered, until chicken meat will easily come off the bones (about 1 hour). Remove the chicken, cool and remove meat from bones. Cut bite-size. Return meat to the pot, bring to a boil and reduce to simmer. Stir the flour into a little water and then stir into the soup. Cook another 10 to 15 minutes or until the soup thickens slightly. Remove bay leaves before serving.

Garnish with the chopped parsley.

Cabbage with Brats or Polish Sausage
(Kohl mit Wurst)

Ingredients to serve 6-8:

1 medium cabbage, shredded
1/8 pound butter or margarine (1/2 stick) melted or 4 T oil
1 onion, peeled and chopped
3 ribs celery, chopped
3 carrots, scraped and sliced
6 cups chicken broth
4 Polish sausages or brats, cooked and sliced (half-inch chunks)
1/3 cup flour
salt and pepper to taste
parsley sprigs for garnish

Sauté the onion and celery in the melted butter a couple minutes or until onion is translucent. Stir in the flour until smooth. Add all other ingredients; bring to a boil; reduce heat to simmer; cook about 15 minutes or until thoroughly heated and carrots are soft.

Garnish with parsley.

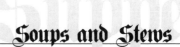

Steak and Wiener Stew *(Rindfleisch und Frankfurter)*

Ingredients to serve 4:

1 lb. round steak (beef, venison or other wild game) cut lean meat into 1 inch squares
1 lb. wieners-cut into 1/2 inch slices
1 cup catsup
1 cup water
1 large sliced onion
salt and pepper
1/2 cup celery, chopped
1/4 cup green pepper, chopped
1/2 cup brown sugar

Place the steak pieces in a large cast iron frying pan. Cover with water. Add a dash each of salt and pepper. Bring to a boil; reduce heat to simmer and cook for 1 hour. Add all other ingredients and simmer for another hour or so until steak is tender.

Serve over boiled potatoes.

Big Game Stew *(Wildragout)**

Ingredients to serve 6-8:

2 pounds roast meat. Bake until tender in a crockpot,*
   then cut into bite-size chunks. (Left-over roast also works well).
Prepare 1/2 cup wild rice by letting it simmer in hot water until well "flowered".

In a large kettle, place:
2 cans vegetable beef stew
1 #2 can tomatoes
1 can mixed vegetables
2 small cans cream of tomato soup
the cooked wild rice
2 tbsp. catsup
Add the meat chunks and heat (about 30 minutes on a medium burner).

*I season the roast with pepper and garlic salt, then sear it in hot oil in a frying pan on both sides (about 1 minute per side). I then place it in a crock pot and add enough water to cover the roast and sprinkle an envelope of dry onion soup mix overall. After two hours I turn the roast over and bake another two hours on low heat.

Small Game Mulligan (Wildragout)*

Use whatever small game is available-squirrel, rabbit, partridge, pheasant, duck, etc. Don't hesitate to mix the game; the greater the variety the better. Cut meat from the bone. Cut into bite-size chunks. Dredge in seasoned flour and brown in oil. Cover with water, season with salt and pepper, and simmer 30 minutes.

Then add the following:

1 #2 can tomatoes (or use fresh tomatoes)
1/2 cup wild rice, uncooked
1/2 cup catsup or two cans tomato soup (or some of each)
1 large onion, sliced
2 beef bouillon cubes
(if no poultry meat is used, use 4 cubes and no chicken bouillon)
2 chicken bouillon cubes
(if no red meat is used, use 4 cubes and no beef bouillon)
2 large carrots, sliced
1 turnip, sliced
3 large potatoes, cubed
1/2 cup celery, chopped
2 tbsp. parsley, chopped

Let simmer 3 hours. Pour off liquid or add water for desired "thickness".
A crock pot works well for this recipe.

*Americanized version. Wild rice is not native to Germany.

German Oven Beef Stew - easy*

Ingredient	Amount	Procedure
Beef stew meat, raw, lean,	2 pounds	Place all ingredients in a larger roasting pan. Cut meat in 1-1/4 thick chunks.
Carrots, peeled, cut in 1-1/4	8 (may add more) inch thick coin shape pieces	You many use a crock pot instead of roasting pan.
Celery, cut in 3/4 inch thick chunks	1 cup	Cover, and bake at 250 degrees for 6 hours
Potatoes, peeled, cut in fourths	4 large	
Onion soup mix, dry	1/2 package	
Tomatoes, diced, canned	One 32 ounce can	
Sherry, cooking	1/2 cup	
Tapioca, dry	3 tablespoon	
Bread, white, crusts removed and cut in 1/2 inch thick cubes	2 slices	
Granulated sugar	1 tablespoon	
Thyme, leaves	1/8 teaspoon	
Marjoram, leaves	1/8 teaspoon	
Rosemary, crushed	1/8 teaspoon	
Salt	1 tablespoon	

* Recipe by Barbara Pappenfus: submitted by Lynn (Pappenfus) Durrenberger

German Cut Bean Stew *(Schnippelbohne)**

Ingredients

Double	Single (Serves 4)
4-6lbs	3lbs. short ribs (beef)
4lbs.	2lbs. fresh green beans diced thin (french cut) (1 lb beans = 4 cups)
2	1 large potato cubed
2	1 large onion sliced
	salt, pepper, bay leaf, fresh green onions, chives, parsley

Sauce:

Double	Single
8	4 strips cut up bacon, fry and reserve drippings
2 tbs	1tbs bacon drippings
4	2 large tbs. flour (rounded)
4 tbs	2 tbs. cider vinegar
4 tsp.	2 tsp. sugar

1. Early in day. Brown short ribs in veg. oil on all sides on medium heat. Season with salt and pepper. Add about 1 qt. water, onion, bay leaf. Bring to boil then simmer 2-1/2 hours till tender. Remove meat and cool broth. Skim fat off. Add beans, potatoes, green onion or chives and cook 20 minutes or just until tender. Reserve (1-2 c. broth)

2. In a separate pan make white sauce: Stir flour into bacon drippings, add some reserved broth. Bring to boil stirring until thick and add cider vinegar, sugar. Adj. seasonings to taste. Add to beans,
add meat, bacon and reheat. Serve with hard rolls and garnish with parsley, chopped.

*Erna Berger's recipe; provided by Joyce Pappenfus, St. Cloud, Minnesota

Notes

Dumplings and Potato Pancakes

Chapter Two

Ingredients to make 12 dumplings:

3 cups raw potatoes, peeled and grated
3 cups mashed potatoes (use leftovers if you have them)
4 T flour
2 eggs
1 T corn starch
1 t salt

Mix together all ingredients. Meanwhile, start water boiling in a large soup kettle
(about 3 quarts of water).

Make 1 dumpling – about the diameter of a half-dollar – and drop into the boiling water. If
the dough starts to disintegrate, it means it is too soft. Add another T of cornstarch. Keep trying
and adding cornstarch until the dumplings hold together. When it is the right consistency,
make all of the dough into half-dollar size dumplings and drop them into the boiling water.
Test after 5 minutes for doneness. May be served with butter or bacon bits or gravy.

Rose Germann's Baseball Dumplings

Ingredients to serve 6 (as a side-dish):

6 large potatoes, peeled, quartered, cooked and mashed
4 slices toast (bite-size pieces)
2 C flour
salt
1/4 pound butter, melted

Boil potatoes, mash and let cool. Using hands, mix potatoes and toast. Mix flour with potatoes to form a ball about the size of a baseball. You may need more flour. Put balls in boiling salted water for 15 to 20 minutes. When they float to the top, use a slotted spoon to take out. Brown butter and pour over balls.

Sometimes Rose would use 1 or 2 eggs and 1 t baking powder.
In memory of Rose Germann, Staples, Minnesota

Charles King's Potato Dumplings with Ham

Bake 1/2 cross cut ham, fully cooked, for 2 hours in a covered roaster. Place the ham on a shallow rack, cut side down. Add 2 inches of water. Optional: After cooking for 1-1/2 hours pour 1 can of beer over ham and resume cooking for 30 minutes. Remove ham and cool before slicing. Cool broth overnight by pouring into kettle and refrigerating or placing roaster in garage (if winter time). Next morning skim off the white fat from the broth. Pour broth into 3 or 4 quart kettle and add 2 quarts of water. Kettle size is large, but that makes cooking the dumplings easier.

Making the Dumplings
Peel 8 medium sized potatoes. Cut the potatoes, by hand, into smaller pieces and then chop in food processor into a grated texture, using large chopping blade. Drain off excessive juice or pat off juice with paper towel. This will cause you to use less flour when making the dumplings, and the dumplings will be lighter. Place grated potatoes in a large mixing bowl. Add one egg, 2/3 tsp. baking powder and 1 tablespoon of salt. Mix and add enough flour so mixture can be made into medium to large dumplings, using a large mixing spoon.

Boiling Dumplings
Bring ham broth to a boil. Dip mixing spoon into broth as you form the dumplings-put in broth and lift dumplings from the bottom of the spoon until they float to the top.

Important
Don't overcook. In about 3-4 minutes, remove and cut one dumpling in half. When done, the center of the dumpling should look porous. If you overcook the dumplings, the centers will get hard and look glazed. Proper cooking of the dumplings is the key to making good dumplings. DON'T OVERCOOK THEM!!!!

Courtesy Charles King, Grand Forks, North Dakota

Filled Dumplings

2 cups flour
1/2 cup milk
1 whole egg and 1 egg yolk
2 tbsp. sour cream
1/2 tsp. salt
2 tbsp. butter

Mix ingredients and knead to a soft pliable dough. Let rest for 10 minutes covered in a warm place. Divide dough in halves and roll thin, cut circles with large biscuit cutter. Place a small spoonful of filling a little to one side. Moisten edges with water, fold over and press edges together firmly. Be sure they are well sealed to prevent the filling from running out. Drop dumplings into salted boiling water. Cook gently for 5 minutes. Lift out of water gently with perforated spoon and serve with melted butter.

Cheese and Potatoes:

1 heaping cup mashed potatoes
1 small cup dry cottage cheese
salt and pepper to taste
few chives or onion, cut fine

Mix thoroughly, but lightly and fill. Serve with melted butter.

Cottage Cheese:

1 cup cottage cheese
1 tsp. melted butter
1 egg, beaten
3 tbsp. sugar
3 tbsp. currants
1 tsp. lemon juice

Blend cheese with melted butter. Add other ingredients and mix well. Fill dumplings. Serve with melted butter and sour cream.

Prune Filling:

1 cup cooked prunes
1 tbsp. sugar
1 tsp. lemon juice

Soak prunes overnight in water. Cook with sugar and lemon juice. When cool remove stones from prunes and fill dumplings. Serve with melted butter and whipping cream.

Ingredients to serve 4:

1-1/2 cups all purpose flour
1/4 cup milk
3 eggs, beaten
1-1/2 t salt
2 quarts water
2 T butter, melted

Combine the first four ingredients. This should result in a fairly "sticky" dough.
Pour the water into a kettle and bring to a boil.
Pour the dough into a colander or sieve that has first been sprayed with a non-stick product.
Force the dough through the colander into the boiling water. A wooden spoon works well for
this purpose. Small pieces of dough will drop into the water. They will be cooked in two or three
minutes and will rise to the surface where they may be scooped out with a slotted spoon.
Add the melted butter and toss.

Ingredients to serve 6:

1 cup milk
3 eggs
3 cups flour (all purpose)
1 t salt
1/2 t nutmeg
2 quarts water to which 1 T salt has been added in which to cook the spaetzel
3 T melted butter to toss with cooked spaetzel

Equipment needed:
sauce pan (approximately 4 quarts)
grater
large wooden spoon
bowl for mixing ingredients
slotted spoon

Beat the eggs and combine with milk, salt and nutmeg. Stir in flour, slowly, until batter adheres to the spoon and is quite stiff. If dough is too stiff, add water one T at a time. Let stand 15 minutes. Meanwhile, bring salted water to a boil.

Using the wooden spoon, press the dough against the grater or through a colander into the boiling water. The spaetzel will cook quickly and come to the surface in two or three minutes. When the surface is well covered, scoop the spaetzel out with the slotted spoon and into a bowl. Repeat until all dough is used up.

When all the spaetzel has been cooked, toss with the melted butter. If the spaetzel has cooled down, re-heat in microwave.

*Courtesy Judy Jenkins, Staples, Minnesota

#1 Enjoy as is with only the melted butter added.
#2 Stir into hot chicken soup.
#3 Serve with your favorite beef stroganoff recipe, or try this one.*

Ingredients to serve 6:

2 pounds good quality, tender steak, cubed
2 T cooking oil
1 T salt
1 t freshly ground pepper
3/4 cup flour (all purpose)
1 large onion, minced
2 T butter
1 clove garlic, minced
2/3 pound fresh mushrooms, chunked
2 cans beef broth (14 oz. size)
4 T catsup
2 T Worcestershire sauce
1/2 t Tabasco or to taste

Combine flour, salt and pepper. Add steak cubes to the bowl and stir until meat is well-coated. Brown steak pieces in hot cooking oil. Add remaining ingredients and simmer 30 minutes or until meat is tender. (Stir occasionally)

*Courtesy Judy Jenkins, Staples, Minnesota

Mashed Potato Pancakes *(Kartoffelpaffer)*

Ingredients for 6 cakes:

3 cups mashed potatoes
1/2 stick butter or margarine, melted
1/2 cup chopped chives
1 egg
2 T cooking oil
2 cloves garlic, peeled and minced

Sauté the garlic in the melted butter 3 or 4 minutes. Combine all ingredients including the butter used to sauté the garlic.
Spoon the potato mixture in 6 portions on a greased griddle or use a skillet. Flatten with a spatula into cakes. Fry over medium heat, brown on both sides.
Serve plain or with butter and/or sour cream.

Potato Pancakes *(Kartoffelpuffer)*

Ingredients to serve 6-8 cakes:

6 large potatoes, peeled and diced
1 small onion, peeled and diced
2 eggs 4 T flour
1/2 t salt
enough cooking oil so that it is about 1/2 inch deep in a skillet

Place the potatoes, onion and eggs in a blender until they have a "grated" appearance. Blend in the flour and salt. Pre-heat the oil in the skillet using a hot burner. Spoon the batter into the skillet, making 6-8 patties; flatten with a spatula. Fry until golden brown on both sides. Serve plain or with butter and/or sour cream.

Ingredients for about 1 dozen pancakes:

(a slightly different recipe)
2 cups grated or finely chopped potatoes
1 cup grated or finely chopped apple (no peel or core)
4 T flour
1 egg
1/2 t salt
1/2 t pepper
oil for frying

Combine grated apple and potato; add and stir in all other ingredients. Pre-heat a generous amount of oil (about 1/4 inch) in a heavy skillet so that the oil is ready when you finish mixing the batter. Using a tablespoon, drop 3 spoonfuls per pancake into the hot oil. Allow about 3 minutes to brown on bottom side, then turn with a spatula; fry until brown on both sides. If the batter is so thick that is does not flatten out on its own when dropped in the oil, gently flatten with a spatula. Option: Sprinkle with confectionery sugar.

Breads
Chapter Three

Black Rye Bread *(Schwarzbrot)*

The dark breads of Europe are very different from traditional American breads. Nothing goes better with cheese!

Ingredients for 2 loaves:

3 cups flour, all-purpose
3 cups rye flour
1/2 cup molasses
2 pkgs. dry yeast
1 T caraway seeds (or cardamom)
2 cups water
2 T butter
2 T sugar
1 t salt
1/4 cup unsweetened cocoa (optional - a modern day touch)

Mix together white flour, cocoa, yeast and seeds. Meanwhile, beat together in a large kettle the molasses, water, salt, sugar and butter and heat until warm.

Combine the two mixtures and beat at slow speed 30 seconds and then 3 minutes at high speed (electric mixer).

Stir in the rye flour. Knead by hand about 5 minutes.

Cover and set in warm place about 30 minutes.

Punch down, and divide, placing in two loaf pans. Make a few slashes in the tops of the loaves with a sharp knife. Cover and let stand in a warm place until the volume doubles (usually a little less than 1 hour).

Bake in a pre-heated 400° oven for about 30 minutes or until done.

Turn out of the pans and let cool on a rack.

Brush tops with butter or oil.

Ingredients for one loaf:

3 cups all purpose flour
1 T baking powder
1 t salt
4 t sugar
1 cn of beer at room temperature (12 oz.)
1/8 stick butter, melted

Combine the first four ingredients, then stir in the beer. Do not over-stir. It is OK if the batter is lumpy. Pour into a loaf pan; brush on the melted butter; place in a pre-heated 375˚ oven. Bake for about 40 minutes or until a toothpick comes out clean.

Rye Bread

Ingredients

1 stick (1/2 cup) margarine
1 cup brown sugar
1/2 cup molasses
2-3/4 cups boiling water
1 t salt
2 pkg dry yeast
1/2 t sugar
1/4 cup warm (110°F) water
1 T anise seed
3 cups rye flour
3-4 cups white flour

Place margarine, brown sugar and molasses in bowl. Pour boiling water over this mixture. Stir in salt. Proof yeast with sugar and water until foamy.
Stir above mixtures together. Add anise seed. Mix in flours. Dough will be sticky until it is completely kneaded. Knead until smooth and elastic, 15-20 minutes. Allow to rise in greased, covered bowl until double in bulk. Punch down and separate dough for loaves. Pat into greased pans; cover and allow to rise until nearly double in bulk. Will be soft to the touch; finger will leave impression. Bake at 350°F 45 minutes. Brush with brown sugar syrup.

Cardamom Bread

Ingredients

4 cups flour
1/4 pound butter
1-1/2 cups milk
1/2 t salt
1 T ground cardamom or 2 T seeds
1/2 cup sugar
1 pkg yeast (2 oz)

Melt the butter. Combine milk and melted butter. Place yeast in mixing bowl and add milk-butter mixture. Add salt, cardamom and sugar. Add flour until a workable dough is formed. Work dough until smooth; let rise 10 minutes (in the bowl). Place dough on a flour-dusted table or board. Shape and cut into loaves or buns. Let rise until dough about doubles in volume.
Brush with a beaten egg.
Bake in a hot oven. Loaves will take 15 to 20 minutes; rolls about half that time.

Saffron Bread

Use the same basic recipe as above (for cardamom breads) but eliminate the cardamom. Use a little more butter and before working in the flour add 1 t ground saffron. Saffron is a potent seasoning; be sure it is mixed in evenly and thoroughly. Experience will teach you how much you would like to use. Make into either loaves or buns.
For variety, add raisins (about 3/4 cup for the above recipe).

German Old Fashioned Cinnamon Rolls *

Ingredient	Amount	Procedure
Evaporated Milk	1 cup Water	Combine 1 cup evaporated milk 3/4 cups and 3/4 cup water in saucepan. Scald milk by heating it over medium temperature until milk comes to rolling boil. Watch carefully so it does not boil over.
Granulated Sugar	1/2 cup plus 2 T	Add sugar, lard (or shortening) and salt to the saucepan containing scalded milk-water mixture. Stir until sugar is dissolved and shortening is melted.
Lard (or shortening) Salt	3/4 cup 1 t	Cool the mixture to lukewarm temperature and pour into large mixing bowl.
Warm Water	1/2 cup	Place warm water in small bowl.
Dry fast rising yeast	3 packages	Sprinkle dry fast rising yeast into bowl containing warm water. Stir until dissolved.
Granulated Sugar	1 teaspoon	Sprinkle sugar on top of yeast-water mixture. Let stand for 10-15 minutes until yeast has risen. Stir yeast mixture into large mixing bowl containing luke warm milk mixture.
Eggs, beaten	2 large	Add the beaten eggs to milk - yeast mixture and beat well.

White all purpose flour *(I use ONLY King Arthur Flour)*	7 1/2 cups	Gradually add and knead in the flour until dough leaves side of bowl. Place in large greased mixing bowl; brush with shortening; let rise in warm place until double in bulk. Turn out of bowl and knead. Stretch dough into a rectangle shape that is 18 inches X 12 inches in size.
Butter, soft Granulated Sugar Cinnamon	1/8 cup 1/2 cup 1/4 cup *(Yes this is right)*	Spread butter evenly over dough. Sprinkle sugar - cinnamon mixture over top. Roll rectangle so it resembles a sausage. Using a sharp knife, cut long roll into 18 slices or rolls.
Large cookie sheets	3	Grease 3 large cookie sheets. Place 6 rolls onto each cookie sheet. Evenly space so rolls do not touch. Using the palm of your hand, SLIGHTLY flatten each cinnamon roll to 3-1/2 inches in diameter. Cover. Let rise until rolls are half again as large. Bake 350 degrees F about 15 minutes or until lightly browned. Spread each roll while still hot with melted better. Cool.

*Recipe by Gertrude Durrenberger; submitted by Lynn (Pappenfus) Durrenberger

Salads
Chapter Four

Ingredients to serve 6:

10 small to medium potatoes, sliced or diced
1 small onion, sliced and broken into rings
3 ribs celery, chopped
6 slices bacon, fried crisp and crumbled
2 cups salad greens
1/2 cup walnuts, chopped
4 T olive or vegetable oil
3 T poppy seeds
2 T lemon juice or cider vinegar
3 T apple juice or cider
1 clove garlic, minced

Cook the sliced or diced potatoes in a covered sauce pan for 20 minutes or until done.
Refrigerate 30 minutes.
Fry bacon until crisp; cool and crumble.
Make a dressing of the last five ingredients. Place all other ingredients in a bowl and gently fold in the dressing until everything is coated. Bacon bits may be used as a garnish or folded into the salad.
Serve hot or cold.

German Style Potato Salad #2

Ingredients to serve 6-8:

10 medium red potatoes, sliced or diced
4 ribs celery, chopped
1 medium to large onion, peeled, sliced and broken into rings
8 bacon strips, fried crisp and broken into bits
2 T vinegar
2 T vegetable oil
3/4 cup sour cream
1/2 t salt
1/4 t pepper
3 T flour

Using a sauce pan, cover the sliced or diced potatoes with water and cook uncovered until done (about 20 minutes).
Fry the bacon strips in a skillet until crisp. Let cool and break into bits. Save the drippings.
Make a dressing by combining the last six ingredients plus 2 T bacon drippings.
Combine all ingredients and gently fold in the dressing. The bacon bits may be used as a garnish or folded into the salad.
Serve hot; this may necessitate re-heating in a skillet or using a microwave.
Serve hot or cold.

German Style Potato Salad #3

Ingredients to serve 6:

10-12 small potatoes, sliced or diced
6 strips bacon, fried crisp then broken into bits
1 medium onion, sliced and broken into rings
1/2 cup wine or cider vinegar
1/2 t salt
1/4 t pepper
3 t chopped parsley for garnish

Using a sauce pan, cover the sliced or diced potatoes with water, then cook covered 20 minutes or until done.
Using a skillet, fry the bacon until crisp. Let cool. Remove bacon and break into bits. Save 2 T of the bacon drippings.
Sauté the onion in 2 T bacon drippings a couple minutes or until the onion is clear.
Place everything in the skillet. Stir gently over low-medium heat until all ingredients are warm (do not let burn).
Garnish with parsley or stir into the salad.
Serve hot or cold.

German Style Potato Salad #4

Ingredients to serve 6-8:

10-12 small, new potatoes, peeled, sliced or diced
1 medium onion, peeled, sliced and broken into rings
3 ribs celery, chopped
1/2 cup chopped sweet green pepper
6 strips bacon, fried and broken into bits
1 T prepared mustard
3 T cider or wine vinegar
3T lemon juice
1 T flour
1/2 t salt
1/4 pepper

Using a covered sauce pan, cover the sliced or diced potatoes with water and cook 20 minutes or until soft. Fry the bacon in a skillet until crisp. Remove, let cool then break into bits. Stir together the mustard, cider or vinegar, lemon juice, flour, salt and pepper. Pour the water off the cooked potatoes and add all ingredients to the sauce pan. Put the pan over low heat and gently stir until all ingredients are hot - but don't let them burn. Serve hot or refrigerate and serve cold.

German Style Potato Salad #5

Ingredients to serve 6:

12 small new potatoes, sliced (with or without skins)
1 medium onion, peeled, sliced thin and broken into rings
4 tbsp. diced green sweet pepper
4 tbsp. diced red pepper
3 tbsp. chopped fresh dill
1/2 cup olive oil
3 tbsp. lemon juice or vinegar
1/2 cup sour cream
pepper to taste
garnish with paprika

Boil the potatoes in a covered saucepan for about 20 minutes or until done.
Gently combine all ingredients. Refrigerate at least 30 minutes before serving.

German Style Potato Salad #6

Ingredients to serve 8:

8-10 medium potatoes
10 slices lean bacon
3 ribs celery, chopped
1 medium to large sweet onion, sliced and rings broken up
1 cup vinegar
1/4 cup water
4 tbsp. flour
1/2 cup sugar
salt and pepper to taste

Fry and crumble the bacon.
If the potatoes are new, leave skins on; if not, peel. Cut potatoes in half and boil until done, but not mushy. Cut into bite-size cubes or slices.
While the potatoes are cooking, mix together in a saucepan all other ingredients except the salt and pepper. Bring to a boil and then reduce heat to simmer - stirring occasionally. When potatoes are done, drained and cubed, pour the liquid over the hot potatoes, add the bacon bits and season with salt and pepper as you gently stir them together. Serve hot.

German Style Potato Salad #7*

Ingredients Serves 8:

10-12 red potatoes (about 4 pounds), scrubbed,
   not peeled, and cut into bite-size
1 pound bacon, cut up and cooked until crisp
1 medium onion, chopped
1 cup celery, chopped
1 medium red pepper, chopped
1/2 cup white wine vinegar
1 tbsp sugar
1/3 cup water
1/2 tsp. salt (or to taste)
1/4 tsp. fresh ground black pepper
1 tbsp. brown style mustard
2 tbsp. parsley, chopped

Cook potatoes in boiling salted water until slightly cooked, but still firm. Drain potatoes. Cook bacon and save 1/2 or more of the grease to cook the onions, (do not drain), then stir in the vinegar, sugar, water, salt, pepper, and mustard and cook for 1 minute. Pour the hot mixture over the chopped vegetables and gently stir together, taste for seasoning. Add the bacon and stir gently. Place in crock pot and cook on low for about 4 hours or more, or place in oven and bake at medium heat for 1 hour. Just before serving, stir the potato salad and top with the parsley.

* Courtesy Joyce Pappenfus; St. Cloud, Minnesota

Ingredients to serve 8:

8-10 medium potatoes
10 slices lean bacon
3 ribs celery, chopped
1 medium to large sweet onion, sliced and rings broken up
1 cup vinegar
3/4 cup water
4 T flour
1/2 cup sugar
salt and pepper to taste

Fry and crumble the bacon.
If the potatoes are new, leave skins on; if not, peel. Cut potatoes in half and boil until done, but not mushy. Cut into bite-size cubes.
While the potatoes are cooking, mix together in a sauce pan all other ingredients except the salt and pepper. Bring to a boil and then reduce heat to simmer, stirring occasionally. When potatoes are done, drained and cubed, pour the liquid over the hot potatoes, add the bacon bits and season with salt and pepper as you gently stir them together. Serve hot or cold.

Cabbage Salad *(Kopfszlat)*

Ingredients for 6 servings:

1 head lettuce
1 medium onion, separated into rings
6 T of your favorite salad herbs. Dill, parsley, chives or basil are all possibilities. (chopped)
4 T wine vinegar (if available, otherwise white)
6 T vegetable or olive oil
1 T sugar

Rinse and shake lettuce. Tear leaves into a large bowl. Add onion rings and chopped herbs. Mix together with vinegar, oil and sugar. Toss together salad and liquids just before serving. Invite guests to add freshly ground pepper to taste.

Old Fashioned Coleslaw*

Ingredients to serve 6:

1 medium head of cabbage, shredded
1 medium or two small onions, chopped fine
1 small green pepper (not essential), seeded and chopped

Dressing ingredients:

7/8 cup of sugar
1 t salt
1 cup salad dressing or mayonnaise (light, if on a fat free diet)
1/2 cup tarragon vinegar

Mix together the cabbage, onions and green pepper (shredded or grated or chopped fine)
Blend the dressing ingredients together.
Combine vegetables and dressing. Refrigerate and serve chilled.

*Courtesy Harriet Dent, Staples, Minnesota

Sweet and Sour Coleslaw

Ingredients to serve 6-8:

1 large head of cabbage, shredded
2 carrots, shredded
1 onion chopped fine
1 rib celery, chopped
1 cup sugar
1/2 cup vinegar
1/2 cup vegetable oil
1/2 t salt
1/2 t pepper

Combine the sugar, vinegar and vegetable oil in a sauce pan. Bring to a boil, stirring regularly. Let cool.
Combine all other ingredients. Stir in sugar-vinegar-oil mixture. Refrigerate and serve chilled.

Apple Coleslaw

Ingredients to serve 8:

6 cups shredded cabbage
3 apples, peeled, cored and diced
1 cup green, seedless grapes (halved if you have time)
1 cup chopped sweet pickles
3 T chopped sweet onion
1 cup mayonnaise or coleslaw dressing (light, if on a fat free diet)
3 T sugar
2 T vinegar
3 T chopped sweet onions

Combine the cabbage, apples, grapes, pickles and onions in a large bowl. In a small bowl, combine the mayo, sugar and vinegar. Stir the contents of the smaller bowl into the contents of the large bowl.

German Cabbage Slaw - Cold or Hot*

Ingredient	Amount	Procedure
Cabbage, shredded	1/2 head	Add cabbage to large mixing bowl and set aside.
Bacon, Diced	1/2 pound	Brown bacon in large 12-14 inch cast iron frying pan. Remove bacon and place in bowl with cabbage.
Onion, minced	1 cup	Add minced onion to bacon. Cook until browned. Stir frequently to prevent burning. Turn off heat.
Vinegar Sugar	6 tablespoons 2 teaspoons	Add vinegar and sugar to large cast iron frying pan containing browned onion. Heat to boiling.
Salt Pepper	To taste To taste	Season with salt and pepper.

For hot slaw: add shredded cabbage and cooked bacon to frying pan containing dressing. Fold ingredients together with a spatula. Cover and cook it until cabbage is translucent. Transfer to a casserole dish and serve immediately.

For cold slaw: pour hot dressing into bowl containing shredded cabbage and cooked bacon. Blend well. Transfer to casserole dish, cover and place in refrigerator until well chilled. Serve with Sauerbraten or pork along with German Fried potatoes.

* Recipe by Alice Altstatt; submitted by Lynn (Pappenfus) Durrenberger

Smoked Salmon Salad *(Geräucherten Lachssalat)*

Ingredients to serve 6:

2 cups smoked salmon, cut into strips
2 cups cooked potatoes, diced
3 T minced green onion (white portion)
1/2 cup olives, pitted and sliced (either black or green or half of each)

Ingredients for salad oil:

2 T olive oil
2 T white vinegar
1 t prepared mustard

Combine salad ingredients and refrigerate at least 1 hour to chill.
Meanwhile, prepare dressing by mixing the three ingredients. Invite guests to add
salad oil as they are served. Also, make available freshly ground black or white pepper.

Spinach Salad with Strawberries

Use your favorite spinach salad recipe and just add the strawberries or use this one.

Ingredients to serve 4:

4 cups spinach leaves, torn
2 cups frozen strawberries, thawed (or fresh, halved)
3 T sugar
1 T sesame seeds
3 T wine vinegar
1/4 t garlic powder
1/3 cup salad oil of your choosing

Combine the spinach leaves, strawberries and sesame seeds. Shake together the oil, garlic powder, vinegar and sugar.

Mix all ingredient together thoroughly and then distribute into the salad bowls.

Apple with Bacon Salad

Ingredient to serve 6:

1 head of lettuce broken/torn into bite-size
2 apples sliced into narrow wedges
6 slices of bacon, broiled until crisp and cut into narrow strips or crumble.
12 T (2 per serving) grated cheese of your choosing
12 T (2 per serving) slivered almonds
Freshly ground pepper

Dressing ingredients:

Use a dressing of your choosing or try this:
1 cup sour cream
1 cup light mayonnaise
4 T catsup (optional)

For a different treatment, sauté the apple slices in butter.

Beet Salad

Ingredients

3 medium pickled beets, chopped
1 apple, peeled, cored and diced
2 potatoes, boiled, cooled and chopped
1 T chopped onion
1 cup sour cream
1 T mustard (prepared)

Combine all ingredients and chill.

Herring Salad (Heringsalat)

Ingredients to serve 6:

2 cups marinated herring, chopped

Marinade ingredients:

2 cup wine (or white vinegar)
1 onion, chopped

Salad ingredients:

2 cups cooked, diced potatoes
1 cup cooked, diced beets (or pickled, sweetened beets)
1 large dill pickle, chopped
2 hard boiled eggs, chopped
3 T white vinegar
1 T prepared mustard
2 T chopped dill

Marinate the herring 48 hours, refrigerated.
Drain herring pieces in a sieve.
Chop vegetables and chill 2 hours. Toss together all ingredients just before serving.
Do not save.

Meats

Chapter Five

Beef Pot Roast in Beer Marinade

Ingredients to serve 6:

4 pound beef rump roast
2 cns beer, preferably dark
1 medium onion, sliced
1 clove garlic, minced
1 bay leaf
1 cup flour
4 slices bacon
Salt and pepper
1 cup vegetable oil

Rub the roast with salt and pepper. Roll the roast in flour. Brown the roast on all sides in vegetable oil in an iron kettle.
Discard the oil. Pour the beer into the iron kettle. Add the minced garlic and bay leaf.
Return the roast to the kettle. Spread the onion rings and bacon strips over the roast.
Place kettle in a pre-heated 250 degree oven. Bake three to four hours until tender, turning the roast at the end of each hour and moving the bacon and onion to the top of the roast each time.

Ingredients to serve 8:

4 pound beef roast
enough butter or oil to brown roast

Marinade Ingredients:

2 cups red wine vinegar
1 large onion, chopped
3 stalks (ribs) celery, chopped
12 peppercorns
1 bay leaf
1 t cloves
1 t caraway seeds

Combine all marinade ingredients in a sauce pan. Bring to a boil; reduce heat and let simmer about 5 minutes. Let cool. Place the roast in a covered container (glass or Tupperware) with the marinade poured over it. Refrigerate and marinate two days, turning whenever you think about it (2 or 3 times each day).

Remove the roast, pat dry and brown in oil or butter in a Dutch oven. Save and strain the marinade, discarding solids. Pour marinade liquid over roast. Cover and cook over low heat until tender.

Marinade and juices from the roast may be used to make a gravy of your choice or may be served on the side and poured over servings of meat.

German Sauerbraten #2*

Ingredient	Amount	Procedure
Vinegar	1-1/2 cups	MARINADE:
Water	1-1/2 cups	Place vinegar, water, bay leaves cloves,
Bay Leaves	2	mace, salt and pepper in a saucepan
Whole Cloves	12	and heat to a rolling boil.
Pepper	1/4 teaspoon	
Mace	1/2 teaspoon	
Salt	1-1/2 teaspoon	
Sugar	1 tablespoon	
Onions, Sliced	3 cups	Place sliced onions in a bowl. Pour hot marinade over the top of the onions.
Cooking Oil (*I use olive oil*)	1 cup	Stir oil into the onion - marinade mixture.
Beef chuck or heel of round	6 pounds	Place beef in a large pan. Pour onion-marinade-oil mixture over the top of the beef. Place pan of beef - marinade mixture in a refrigerator for 3-4 days so it will pickle evenly. Be sure to turn meat after the first 2 days to allow it to pickle well on both sides.

| Lard *(I use olive oil)* | 1/2 cup | Melt lard (or olive oil) in a large Dutch oven. Add meat and brown evenly on both sides. When brown add 2 cups strained marinade. Cover and bring to a boil then reduce to simmer. Cook until tender. Serve with steamed red cabbage and potatoes. |

*Recipe by Maze Durrenberger; submitted by Lynn (Pappenfus) Durrenberger

Marinated Rabbit (Hasenpfeffer)

Ingredients to serve 4:

2 snowshoe or cottontail rabbits
1/2 cup cooking oil
1 cup cooking wine
2 onion, sliced
1 T allspice
1 t salt, a couple of dashes of pepper
1/4 cup flour
2 T sugar

Cut the rabbits into pieces as you would a chicken. Make a marinade of the oil, wine, onions, allspice, salt and pepper. Cover meat; cover dish; refrigerate and marinate for two days. Drain on paper towel, but save marinade. Dredge meat in seasoned flour and brown in cooking oil. Remove rabbit and pour off all oil and fats. Return meat to pan and cover with marinade, adding sugar. Bring to a boil, then reduce heat and simmer until tender (about 45 minutes to 1 hour).

Rabbit (Hasenpfeffer) #2

Prepared in a crockpot

Ingredients to serve 4:

4 pounds dressed rabbit, disjointed and divided into 8 pieces
1 cup chopped celery
1 cup chopped carrots
1 medium onion, chopped
8 slices bacon
2 or more cups red wine
1 t each of dried basil, peppercorns, whole allspice, cloves and dried thyme

Place all ingredients except the pieces of rabbit in a crockpot. Stir together.

Add the pieces of rabbit. If the wine and other ingredients don't come up at least half way on the pieces of rabbit, add more wine or water. Lay the slices of bacon over the rabbit but out of the liquid.

Cook on high two hours, then turn the pieces of rabbit over, again laying the slices of bacon on top of the meat. Continue cooking another two hours, then turn down to low for at least another two hours, or longer if you are not ready to serve.

Serve all ingredients together in shallow bowls.

Potato Sausage *

Ingredients
3 pounds ground pork (lean)
2 pounds lean ground beef
10 pounds potatoes
2 T pepper
5 T salt
1-1/2 t allspice (ground)
1-1/2 t ginger
1/2 pound casings

Soak casings in water to soften and remove salt. Peel and grind potatoes, using medium blade. Add meat and seasonings. Mix well. Tie end of casing and loosely fill in 24" lengths - tie open ends. (The sausage expands when cooked). Keep covered with water. Prick in several places before cooking. Simmer for 30-45 minutes. Drain off water and sauté slowly until browned. Uncooked potato sausage may be frozen in airtight zip-locked bags. Exposure to air causes the potatoes to discolor.

*Courtesy Karen Anderson Cowie, Gull Lake, Brainerd, Minnesota

Meat Roll

Flank meat or other relatively thin "sheets" of meat that can be rolled are usually used. Meat scraps that would normally be used for stew meat (or hamburger) are also used (not tough pieces however). All meat should be boneless.

Lay the flank meat flat. Spread the scraps (bite-sized) evenly over the flank meat. Season lightly with salt and pepper. Sprinkle 1/3 tsp. ginger to each pound of meat. Chop a large onion and sprinkle over meat. Roll and wrap tightly with string.

Prepare a brine solution with enough water to cover the meat. Use enough salt to float an egg or a potato. Add 1/2 tsp. saltpeter per gallon of water. Boil until the salt dissolves.

When the brine has cooled, place the meat roll in non-metallic container and cover with the solution. Place a weight on top to keep the meat totally submerged. Let soak in cool place 48 hours. Remove and soak overnight in fresh water in a cool place.

Remove and place in fresh water again and boil slowly for two hours.
Place meat in loaf pan; force to fit. Use more than one pan and cut meat to fit if necessary. Store in cool place with weight on top to hold shape.
Slice thin and serve cold.

Head Cheese

**This tasty delicacy receives its name from the fact the pork used tradition-
ally came from a hog's head. You may still use that source for this recipe,
but hog's head may be a little hard to come by in your local market!**

Ingredients

2 pounds shank or beef roast
2 pounds pork shoulder roast or lean meat from a hog's head
10 allspice
5 bay leaves
1 tsp. garlic salt
1 tsp. white pepper
3 tbsp. brown sugar
2 onions, sliced (medium)
2 tbsp. salt

Chop both the beef and the pork into small pieces (about 1/2 bite-size).
Place in a crockpot and cover with water. Let simmer on low until very tender (about 4-5 hours).
Place the meat in a dishtowel; tie with a string; and place in a stone crock or other
non-metallic container.
Make a spice-brine by adding the spices and brown sugar as listed above to enough water
to cover the meat. Boil briefly, stirring continuously. Pour the solution over the meat.
Place a board on top of the meat and press down firmly. Place a clean rock on top of the
board to maintain pressure.
Store in a cool place or under refrigeration. Wait a couple of days and then slice cold to serve-
with vinegar on the side.

Ingredients for 6 servings:

1/2 cup rice
1 cup onion, chopped
1 head cabbage, medium
1-1/2 pounds ground beef
1-1/2 cups tomato juice
1 T Worcestershire sauce
1 T sour cream (from the dairy case)
salt and pepper

Cook the rice. Wash the cabbage. Take out the center core. Place the head in hot water until the leaves start to loosen or become limp. Carefully separate off a dozen of the larger leaves. Mix together the hamburger, rice, onion, sour cream, Worcestershire sauce and season lightly. Place about a third of a cup of the mixture on each leaf, as far as it will go. Roll up in each cabbage leaf and pin with toothpicks. Cover the bottom of the baking dish with cabbage leaves and then lay the cabbage rolls on this bed of leaves. Pour the tomato juice over the cabbage rolls and place in a 325° oven. Bake for about one hour and fifteen minutes. Remove the rolls and place on a serving platter. Pour the tomato juice over the rolls. If you wish, you may thicken the juice by stirring in a little flour.

Ingredients to serve 4:

4 steaks of your choosing (cheaper cuts work well)
4 large, yellow onions, peeled and chopped (not too fine)
1 stick (quarter pound) butter
Salt and pepper to taste
Vegetable oil
Chopped chives for garnish

Tenderize the steaks by pounding them with a mallet made for that purpose or use the but end of a table knife or similar instrument. Avoid using a knife with a sharp blade.

Melt the butter in a heavy frying pan (cast iron works well) and sauté the onions over medium heat; season them with salt and pepper. Remove onions and add a thin layer of vegetable oil to the frying pan. Fry the steaks over high heat, about 5 minutes on each side. Return the onions to the frying pan during the last minute or two of frying. Serve the steaks covered with the caramelized onions and garnish with the chopped chives.

Beef Tenderloin with Glaze (mit Glasun)

Ingredients for 8 servings:

5 pounds beef tenderloin - all fat removed
1 pound fresh mushrooms (of your choosing)
2 pounds baby carrots
3 pounds small potatoes, preferably new
1/4 cup sherry (preferably cooking sherry)
2 tbsp. cooking oil
1 tsp. lemon pepper
1 tsp. thyme
1 tsp. rosemary
1 tbsp. lemon juice
salt to taste

Sauté the mushrooms in the vegetable oil until they curl. Pre-cook the potatoes (skins on if new) and carrots in boiling water about 10 minutes. Do not over-cook. Should be able to pierce with fork but with difficulty.

Place loin on an oiled rack in a roasting pan. Tuck under the smaller end of the loin if necessary for even thickness. Sprinkle the seasonings (including lemon juice) evenly over the loin. Brush on the sherry (and brush again every 10 minutes).

Bake at 400˚ for 20 minutes and another 10 minutes at 350˚.

Place mushrooms, carrots and potatoes around the loin. Brush the vegetables with the sherry. Bake another 10 to 15 minutes or until the vegetables are tender. If you are using a meat thermometer - until 140˚ for rare or 160˚ for medium.

German Dressing (stuffing)*

Ingredient	Amount	Procedure
Bacon Liver and Gizzards Onion	1 pound From one turkey 2 cups	Run the bacon, livers, gizzard and onion through a grinder. Brown the ground bacon, liver, gizzard and onion in a large 12-14 inch cast iron frying pan.
Celery	5 long leaves (do not use whole stalk of celery-use only 5 leaves)	Run the celery through a grinder. Add the ground celery to the large cast iron frying pan containing the browned bacon, liver, gizzards and onion and brown well.
Butter Sage Salt Pepper	1/4 pound 1 teaspoon 1/2 teaspoon 1/4 teaspoon	Add the butter, sage, salt and pepper to the browned ingredients.
White Bread cut in cubes	From a 1-1/2 pound loaf	Over a 2 hour period AND over low heat very gradually fold the bread cubes into the browned mixture. Be sure to brown slowly to ensure even browning of the bread. This dressing is never mushy. On the contrary it is light, fluffy and simply delicious served with turkey, chicken or pork.

*Courtesy Lynn (Pappenfus) Durrenberger

Goose with Sausage Stuffing (Gans mit füllung)

Ingredients to serve 8:

1 very large goose
(12 pounds or larger; there
is much waste in the carcass)
salt and pepper
Ingredients for the dressing:
2 cups celery, chopped
2 cups onion, chopped
4 cups croutons, pre-seasoned
2 cups sausage, crumbled

1 cup raisins
1 cup water chestnuts
1/2 pound melted butter or margarine
1 cup hot water
1/2 t pepper
1/2 t salt
1 t poultry seasoning
oil or butter to sauté onion and celery

Clean the goose, inside and out. Remove visible fat. Season inside and out with salt and pepper. If the goose is very fat, parboil it for 30 minutes. Prepare the stuffing. Sauté the onion and celery pieces. Brown the crumbled sausage. Melt the butter or margarine. Combine all the dry ingredients. Add the onion and celery, melted butter and hot water. Stir thoroughly. Stuff the goose loosely. Place the balance of the stuffing in foil packages. Roast these packages separate from the goose. Place the goose in a covered roaster and bake at 350° for one hour. Turn oven down to 275° and roast until the drumsticks and wings "wiggle" freely. (usually about 3 more hours) The stuffing in the goose may be too fat to use; if so, discard it. If not too fat, mix thoroughly with stuffing baked separately.

Goose with Sauerkraut Stuffing

Use the previous recipe but stuff with 2 pounds of saurkraut.

Meats 93

German Dutch Oven Dinner*

Ingredient	Amount	Procedure
Lard or shortening Beef, chuck, boneless,	1/2 cup	Place large cast iron Dutch oven on stove burner. Put lard in Dutch oven and melt on medium temperature. Place beef in bottom of heated Dutch oven containing melted fat. Brown slowly on both sides.
Water	2 cups	Add 2 cups water.
Onion, medium size, peeled, cut in half	4	Place onions over browned beef.
Garlic, cloves, fresh, cut in thin slices	6	Sprinkle with garlic, thyme, marjoram rosemary, salt and pepper. Cover the Dutch oven and cook beef and onions slowly on low temperature until beef is very tender, adding more water along the way to prevent beef and onions from sticking and burning.
Thyme, leaves	1/8 teaspoon	
Marjoram, leaves	1/8 teaspoon	
Rosemary, crushed	1/8 teaspoon	
Salt	1/2 teaspoon	
Pepper	1/4 teaspoon	

Potatoes, peeled,	6 small, whole	Arrange potatoes on bottom of Dutch oven. Place beef on top of potatoes.
Carrots, peeled, cut in 2 inch chunks	2 pounds	Layer carrots over beef.
Salt	1/8 teaspoon	Sprinkle with salt and pepper.
Pepper	1/16 teaspoon	
Water	1 cup	Add 1 cup water.
Additional water added along the way to prevent burning		Cover Dutch oven and cook dinner slowly on low temperature for about an hour or more until carrots and potatoes are done. Be sure to add additional water along the way, as needed, to prevent burning of meat and vegetables. When dinner is done, transfer it to a platter and serve. Serve with green salad and hot biscuits.

*Recipe from Lynn (Pappenfus) Durrenberger; submitted by Barbara Pappenfus

Mashed Potatoes on Brats

Ingredients to serve 4:

8 brats or wieners, sliced length-wise
2 large potatoes, peeled and chunked
8 T grated or shredded cheese (cheddar works well)
1/2 cup milk
2 T butter or margarine, melted
salt and pepper to taste

Boil the chunked potatoes in water in a covered sauce pan for about 20 minutes or until done. (check with fork) Drain and return to the stove for a couple of minutes to dry the potatoes.
Slice the brats or wieners length-wise but leave the halves attached with a little skin.
Mash the potatoes, milk and butter together.
Spoon the mashed potatoes on top of the brats or wieners. Season lightly with salt and pepper. Sprinkle with the cheese. Bake in a pre-heated 375° oven for about 15 minutes or until the cheese melts.

Goose or Duck Gravy

While bird is roasting, cook giblets (heart, gizzard and liver) by simmering in water until tender-about 1 hour.

Chop giblets.

Remove bird from roaster.

Skim off the excess fat.

Using a spatula, carefully scrape loose the particles from the bottom of the pan. Do not scrap so hard as to loosen severely burned materials.

Using a pint jar with a cover as a shaker, add 1/2 cup water and 1/4 cup flour. Shake well. If a covered jar is not available, use a bowl, add flour and a little water to make a smooth paste. Now add the rest of the water and stir until the mixture is uniform and there are no lumps. Remove roaster from heat. Add chopped giblets. Slowly stir in the flour and water mixture. Place roaster on low heat on top of stove and allow to simmer, stirring all the while. When the gravy is bubbling all over the roaster, add one tbsp. of Kitchen Bouquet and salt and pepper. Continue to stir over heat for another five minutes and serve. For thicker gravy, add more flour and water mixture.

Parboiled Ducks or Geese *(Ente Oder Gans)*

Tough old ducks or geese will be made both tasty and tender by this technique. Let ducks or geese stand in salted water overnight, breast down (refrigerated).

Place birds in kettle, breasts down, cover with salted water. Bring to a boil; remove after about five to ten minutes of boiling. If you have reason to believe birds are tough, leave a little longer. Remove ducks or geese from kettle, wash off any grease residue, salt and pepper inside and out. Place ducks or geese in roaster, breast up, with a strip of bacon over each breast.

Place in pre-heated 250° oven and bake for another three hours.

Remove cover last half hour to brown. Orange sauce, orange marmalade or honey glaze may be added at this time (remove bacon).

This technique is guaranteed to tenderize even the toughest old Greenhead!

Onion Soup Mix for Tough Old Birds

Fillet and dissect the duck, pheasant or goose and skin.

Do not season.

Lay pieces on foil in a single layer.

Place a generous pat of butter or margarine on each piece (about 1/4 pound per bird). Add about 2 tbsp. water.

Pour the dry onion soup mix over the meat pieces (one envelope for ducks or pheasant; two envelopes for a larger goose).

Fold the foil over the ducks and seal on top with your fingers.

Place in pre-heated 325° oven, sealed side up, for an hour and 15 minutes.

The soup mix liquid may be used as a gravy. Simply pour in bowl and add an equal amount of hot water.

Ducks, geese, or pheasants you have had in the freezer for a long time are ideal candidates for this recipe.

Cheese-Coated Perch

Ingredients:

1 pound fresh perch fillets (or other freshwater fish), remove skin and bones
1/4 cup all purpose flour
1 beaten egg
1 tsp. salt
dash pepper
1/4 cup fine dry bread crumbs
1/4 cup grated Parmesan cheese
1/4 cup shortening
1 eight ounce can tomato sauce
1/2 tsp. sugar
1/2 tsp. dried basil leaves, crushed

Cut fish into serving size portions. Coat with flour and dip into a mixture of egg, salt and pepper, then dip into a mixture of bread crumbs and cheese. Fry fish slowly in a skillet or hot shortening until browned on one side. Turn and brown other side. Combine tomato sauce, 1/4 cup water, sugar and basil in a saucepan. Simmer 10 minutes and serve with the fish.

Baked Northern Pike with Raisin Stuffing

This recipe also works well with other large fish. On the other hand, all fish are not good baked; even the tasty walleye or the flavorful bass are only fair unless they receive special treatment and seasonings. Northerns should weigh four pounds or more, whitefish, walleyes and bass, at least three.

Preparing the fish:

Scale and gut the fish; remove the head, tail and all fins.
Wash and dry the fish, inside and out.
Score the back of the fish with cross-section cuts about three inches apart-down to the backbone.
Salt and pepper, inside and out and in the cuts.

Preparing the stuffing:

1 cup raisins
1/4 lb. butter (added to one cup hot water)
2 cups croutons or dry bread crumbs
1 large onion, chopped but not too fine
salt and pepper
1 cup chopped bologna (or wieners or polish sausage or luncheon meat or breakfast meat)

Place the croutons, raisins, meat and onions in a bowl. Salt and pepper lightly while stirring the ingredients together.

Add and stir in the butter-hot water mixture just before stuffing the fish.

Lay a sheet of foil on the bottom of the roaster.

Stuff the fish (loosely) and place upright on the sheet of foil.

Fold the foil up along both sides of the fish - do not cover the back. The foil will hold in the stuffing. If your fish is too long for the roaster, you may cut it in two and bake the two sections side by side.

Leftover stuffing or additional stuffing may be baked in a foil package alongside the fish or even outside the roaster.

Place a strip of bacon and a slice of onion, alternately, over each score (or cut).

Cover the roaster and place in a pre-heated, 300° oven. After one hour, remove cover and continue to bake until the meat becomes flaky and separates from the backbone (as viewed from the end of the fish). This should take about another half-hour, depending on the size of the fish.

Transfer the baked fish to a platter. Cut through the backbone at each score mark, separating the fish into serving-size portions. The stuffing may be lifted out with each portion as it is served. Serve with tartar sauce and/or lemon.

Fillets in Beer Batter

Fillets should be about 1/2 inch thick and 6 inches long. Skin and remove bones.
Pour one-half cup of beer into a bowl and let stand overnight or until "flat".
Add the beer and a tbsp. of cooking oil to two cups of white flour. Mix.
Beat the whites of three eggs until stiff and work them into the batter.
If mixture is too heavy, add a little water or more beer.
Dip the fillets into the batter and deep fry in very hot cooking oil until golden brown. Turn fillets over once. The batter tends to insulate the fish so make certain they are done before serving.

Beer Batter Recipe #2

Ingredients for one pound of fillets*:

1 cup flour (complete pancake mix works well)
1 cup beer
1 egg
1 t baking powder
1 t salt
1 t garlic salt
1 t lemon pepper

Beat an egg into the beer, then add the flour and other ingredients. The batter should be thick enough so that it sticks to the pieces of fish. If it runs off the fish it is too thin.

Fry in about an inch of hot oil. Turn each piece over once it is brown on the bottom side so that both sides are a rich brown (a little crispy). Serve with white tartar sauce.

*Fillets should be fairly thin - about 1/2 inch thick and no more than 6 inches long.
 Skin and remove bones.

Fish Coated with Cracker Crumbs

Using a rolling pin, crush salted crackers into fine crumbs. Stir in a generous portion of lemon pepper. Prepare an egg wash by beating an egg (more if you are frying a lot of fish) into 2 cups of water.
Skin and remove bones.
Dip the fillets into the egg wash, then into the cracker crumbs and fry in a well oiled hot skillet, browning both sides.

Fish Patties

Chop two cups of flaked, boneless fish-either raw or cooked fish may be used. Almost any kind of fish works just fine. This is a very good way to use-up leftovers. Combine the chopped fish with:

Ingredients

1 egg
1/2 cup chopped onion
pinch or two of salt
1 tsp. lemon pepper
1/2 cup chopped green pepper

Add water to 1 cup "complete" pancake mix until it has the consistency you would use to make pancakes. Add the batter to the fish and other ingredients until it has the consistency (looks like) potato salad.
Drop large spoonfuls on a hot, greased grill or large, non-stick frying pan, forming patties.
Fry until well-browned on both sides. Serve with tartar sauce.

Ingredients:

8 crappies or sunfish, dressed (scale and remove heads, entrails, tails and fins; and drain.)
Cover bottom of baking dish with 1/4 cup finely chopped parsley and arrange the fish in the baking dish.

Top with:

2 tbsp. finely chopped parsley
2 tbsp. chopped fresh dill or
1 tsp. dill seed

Pour 1/4 cup hot water around the fish. Bake at 350° for 20 to 25 minutes and serve.

Vegetables

Chapter Six

Cabbage Strudel

Ingredients for about 16 one inch servings:

3 cups cabbage, thinly sliced
1/2 cup onion, chopped
2 T butter, melted
4 T raisins
1 t caraway seed
1 t cardamom seeds
4 T chicken broth
1/2 t salt
1/2 t pepper, freshly ground
oil to sauté onion
5 sheets filo pastry, thawed out

Sauté onion until clear. Add cabbage, both kinds of seeds and the chicken broth. Bring to a boil, then reduce heat and let simmer - covered - until cabbage is cooked. Stir in raisins, salt and pepper, being careful to distribute seasoning uniformly throughout. Arrange one piece of pastry sheet on a floured board or dish towel. Brush with melted butter. Lay another sheet on top and brush with butter; also a third sheet. Distribute half the mixture along the short side of the pastry sheets (about 1 inch from the edge). Roll tightly and place on cookie sheet. Brush with melted butter. Repeat with remaining pastry sheets and mixture. Bake in a medium oven about 20 minutes or until a golden brown. Cut into one-inch pieces to serve. Left over pieces may be refrigerated for a day or two, but warm before serving.

Ingredients

1 large head red cabbage (2-2.5 lbs. or 6 cups)
1/2-3/4 cup water. Shred cabbage 1/4 in with #4 disk
2 or 3 med. cooking apples (unpeeled and cut into small chunks)
2 or 3 tbsp bacon drippings (or lard)
2 tbsp brown or white sugar
1/2 tsp salt
1/2 tsp allspice + 3 cloves

Cover and simmer 1.5-2 hours till tender. Add 1/3-1/2 cup red wine just before serving
(burgundy or tawny port)

*Erma Berger's recipe; submitted by Char Berger.

Ingredients to serve 6:

1 large red cabbage (about three pounds)
3 apples (medium to large) hard, red variety
1 1/2 cups red vinegar (preferably wine vinegar)
1 T salt
6 cloves
2 cups water
1 T cooking oil
2 T sugar
salt and pepper

Shred cabbage. Core and chop apples. Combine cabbage, apples, vinegar, salt and cloves in a bowl. Cover and let stand over-night. Add cooking oil to a large kettle and heat. Pour cabbage mixture into the pot, then stir in the water and sugar. Simmer until tender. Season with salt and pepper to taste. Serve hot or cold.

"Doctored" Sauerkraut

Ingredients to serve 4:

2 cans sauerkraut (16 oz. each)
1 cup wine (preferably white)
1/2 cup brown sugar (this may vary according to taste - from none to 1 cup)
1 onion, peeled and chopped
1 T cooking oil
1 hard apple, cored and chopped
1 potato (medium plus) peeled and chopped
4 cloves

Sauté the chopped onion in cooking oil until brown. Drain the sauerkraut and add to the pot, sauté a few more minutes, stirring all the while. Add all other ingredients and simmer about 40 minutes. Serve hot or cold.

German Hot Cabbage #3*

Ingredient	Amount	Procedure
Cabbage, shredded Salt Water	1 medium head 1 tablespoon 1 quart	Place shredded cabbage in very large kettle with salt and 1 quart water. Cover and simmer for 2 hours. Remove 2 cups of the cabbage liquid and use to cook potato. Drain off remaining liquid.
Bacon, diced	1/2 pound	Fry diced bacon until brown and crisp and set aside.
Grated Potato	1 large	Place grated potato in saucepan with 2 cups of the cabbage liquid (above) and cook until thick. Add cooked thickened potato, browned bacon and bacon fat to cooked cabbage.
Salt Pepper	1/8 teaspoon 1/16 teaspoon	Season with salt and pepper
		Serve with pork or beef and fried potatoes or hot potato salad.

* Recipe by Hermina (Minnie) Pappenfus; submitted by Lynn (Pappenfus) Durrenberger.

Creamy Mashed Potatoes

Ingredients to serve 6:

6 large potatoes, peeled and chucked
3/4 cup heavy cream
1/2 stick butter or margarine, melted
4 T chopped chives or green onion (both white and green parts)
1 T chopped fresh thyme
1/2 t salt
1/4 t pepper

Boil the chunked potatoes in water in a covered sauce pan for 20 minutes or until done, check with a fork. Drain and then return to the stove a couple of minutes to dry the potatoes. Mash together all ingredients. Use a hand masher or electric mixer.

Ingredients to serve 4:

4 large potatoes, peeled and chunked
1 medium onion, peeled, sliced and broken into rings
1/2 cup milk
1/2 cup sour cream
1/2 stick butter or margarine, melted
1/2 t salt
1/2 t pepper

Boil the potato chunks for about 20 minutes in a covered sauce pan - check with a fork. Drain and return to the stove a couple of minutes to dry. Meanwhile, sauté the broken onion rings in the butter. Let cook until the onions turn brown (but do not burn). Mash together all ingredients, including the butter used to sauté the onion. Use a hand masher or electric mixer. A half-can of French fried onions may be substituted for the fresh onion.

Mashed Potatoes with Blue Cheese

Ingredients to serve 4:

4 large potatoes, peeled and chunked
1/3 cup blue cheese, crumbled
1/3 cup milk
1 small onion, peeled and chopped
1/2 stick butter or margarine, melted
1/2 t salt
1/4 t pepper

Boil the potatoes in a sauce pan, covered, for about 20 minutes or until done – check with a fork. Drain and return to the stove a couple of minutes to dry the potatoes. Mash together all ingredients; use a hand masher or electric mixer. If you really like blue cheese, try a little more than 1/3 cup.

German Fried Potatoes*

Ingredient	Amount	Procedure
Raw potatoes, peeled and sliced 1/8 inch thick slices	3 pounds	Prepare the sliced potatoes and sliced onions and set aside
Onions, sliced 1/8 inch thick slices	2 cups	
Lard (*I use olive oil*)	1/2 cup	Melt lard (or olive oil) in a 12-14 inch cast iron frying pan. Add sliced potatoes and sliced onion to the heated oil in the cast iron frying pan.
Dry Ground Mustard Dried Dill Weed Ground Black Pepper Salt	2 teaspoons 1 teaspoon 1/2 teaspoon 1 teaspoon	Add the ground dry mustard, dried dill weed, black pepper and salt to the cast iron frying pan containing the oil, potatoes and onion. Gently fold all ingredients together with a spatula. Cook UNCOVERED on medium heat for about 45 minutes or until potatoes and onions are brown and tender. Periodically turn potatoes with a spatula to prevent sticking to the bottom of the pan. DO NOT STIR AND DO NOT COVER. Serve with pork or beef.

* Recipe by Cyril Durrenberger; submitted by Lynn (Pappenfus) Durrenberger.

German Wilted Lettuce *

Ingredient	Amount	Procedure
Leaf Lettuce, cleaned and gently torn in large pieces.	4 quarts	Add cleaned and torn lettuce to large mixing bowl and set aside.
Bacon, Diced	4 strips	Brown bacon in large 12-14 inch cast iron frying pan. Remove bacon and place in bowl with lettuce.
Onion, Minced	1/4 cup	Add minced onion to bacon. Cook until browned. Stir frequently to prevent burning. Turn off heat.
Vinegar Sugar	6 tablespoons 2 teaspoons	Add vinegar and sugar to large cast iron frying pan containing browned onion.
Salt Pepper	1/8 teaspoon 1/16	Pour hot onion-vinegar sugar mixture over the lettuce and bacon. Season with salt and pepper. Gently toss all ingredients together. DO NOT OVER-MIX IT WILL CAUSE LETTUCE TO BREAK DOWN AND GET MUSHY. Serve IMMEDIATELY. This is good with beef or pork and hot potato salad or fried potatoes.

* Recipe by Barbara Pappenfus; submitted by Lynn (Pappenfus) Durrenberger

Ingredients to serve 4:

1 cup pickled herring, chopped very fine
2 cups small boiled potatoes, sliced thin
4 slices rye bread, buttered
enough leaf lettuce to cover bread

Butter the bread, top with lettuce, then potato slices, then herring.
Mayonnaise may be used instead of butter.

Casseroles

Chapter Seven

Fish and Potato Casserole

Ingredients to serve 4:

2 pounds of fillets. Almost any variety, but salmon and lake trout
are especially good. Skin and remove bones.
6 potatoes, sliced
Butter, enough to butter the casserole dish
3 tbsp. chopped dill or 2 tbsp. dill seed
salt and pepper
6 eggs
1 pint of milk (2 cups)

Butter the casserole dish. Place a layer of sliced potatoes on the bottom. Next a layer of fillets. Lightly season the fillets with salt and pepper. Sprinkle lightly with the dill. Add another layer of potatoes then a layer of fish, more seasonings, etc. making sure the top layer is potatoes. Beat the eggs and milk together and pour over all. Bake in a low oven (250°) for about 1 hour or until potatoes are done.

Tunafish Casserole

Ingredients:

1 standard size can of tuna
1 onion (medium) chopped quite fine
2 tbsp. chopped green pepper
1 can mushroom soup
1 cup cheese (Velveeta or similar)
2 eggs
1/2 package egg noodles (8 oz.)

Cook egg noodles in water according to package directions. Mix together all ingredients, place in a greased casserole dish, and bake for 45 minutes in a pre-heated 350° oven.

Potato and Sausages Casserole

Ingredients to serve 4:

2 pounds potatoes (red, white, yellow - not russets)
1 pound sausages, sliced (wieners or bologna also work well)
1/2 pound shredded cheese (cheddar works well)
2/3 cup water
1 cup milk
3 T flour
3 T butter
2 bouillon cubes

Boil potatoes until tender (check with a fork); set aside and let cool; then slice. Lubricate a baking dish with butter or shortening. Layer the potato and sausage slices alternately. Melt butter, then add water, milk, flour and bouillon cubes. Heat and stir until cubes are dissolved. Pour contents over potatoes and sausage slices, sprinkle with shredded cheese. Bake in a pre-heated 400° oven for 30 minutes.

Potato and Cabbage Casserole

Ingredients to serve 4:

1 small head cabbage (about 2 pounds) de-cored and sliced thin
2 pounds potatoes (not russets). Peel, boil until tender, slice thin.
10 slices thick bacon, fried; discard grease
1/2 pound butter (divided)
1 cup milk
1/3 cup flour
salt and pepper

Boil cabbage slices in water until tender (about 10 minutes). Boil potato slices in water until tender (about 15 minutes). Cut bacon into small pieces, fry, discard grease. Melt butter. In a sauce pan, place half the melted butter and all of the flour and milk. Season with salt and pepper. Cook, stirring all the while, until it thickens. Place half the cabbage, potatoes and bacon in a greased baking dish. Pour half the sauce over the contents. Add the remainder of the cabbage, potatoes and bacon and pour the remaining sauce over contents. Drizzle the remaining butter over all. Bake in a pre-heated 400° oven for 20 minutes.

Eintopfgerichte

Sauerkraut and Sausage Casserole

Ingredients to serve 4:

2 cans (16 oz. or thereabouts) sauerkraut
1 package of noodles (8 oz.)
1 pound sausages (or more if your guests are real "meat-eaters")
of your choosing (sliced)
1 cup water
4 T brown sugar
sour cream (optional)

Drain the sauerkraut. Add water and brown sugar to the sauerkraut and simmer in a pot 30-40 minutes. Meanwhile, prepare the noodles according to the directions on the package. Combine all of the ingredients in a baking (casserole) dish and top with sour cream (optional). Bake in a pre-heated 350° oven for 40 minutes.

Ingredients to serve 4:

1 8 oz. package spaghetti
1 pound sausages of your choice, sliced (wieners or bologna also work well)
3 tomatoes, sliced
1 cup shredded cheese of your choosing
2 eggs
1/2 cup milk

Cook the spaghetti according to the directions on the box. In a baking dish, combine the spaghetti, sausage and tomatoes. Beat the eggs in the milk and pour over contents of the casserole. Scatter cheese on top. Bake in a pre-heated 350° oven for 30 minutes.

Scalloped Potatoes with Ham

Ingredients to serve 8:

8 medium potatoes, peeled and sliced
1-1/2 pounds of ham, diced
1 can cream of celery soup
1 can cream of onion soup
1-1/2 cups milk
1 cup cheddar cheese, grated or shredded
salt and pepper to taste

Arrange the sliced potatoes in layers in a lightly greased flat baking dish or pan. Use a large enough pan so that there are no more than 2 or 3 layers. Combine the two cans of soup with the milk and ham. Pour evenly over the potatoes - redistributing some of the ham if necessary. Sprinkle lightly with salt and pepper. Sprinkle the cheese evenly, over contents of dish. Bake covered in a pre-heated 350° oven 1 hour. Take off cover and bake another 15 minutes or until potatoes are tender.

Scalloped Potatoes with
Tomatoes and Wieners or Brats

Ingredients to serve 6-8:

8 medium potatoes, peeled and sliced
1 can cream of celery soup
1 can cream of onion soup
2 cups milk
3 tomatoes, sliced fairly thin
1 pound wieners or brats, sliced bite-size
1-1/2 cups Swiss cheese, shredded or grated
salt and pepper to taste

Arrange the sliced potatoes in layers in a lightly greased flat baking dish or pan. Combine the soups, milk and wiener slices and pour evenly over the potatoes. You may have to rearrange the wiener pieces. Lightly season with salt and pepper. Sprinkle the cheese, evenly, over the potatoes. Bake, covered, one hour in a pre-heated 350° oven. Uncover and bake another 15 minutes or until potatoes are tender. Arrange tomato slices over the contents.

Cheesy Vegetarian Casserole

Ingredients to serve 6:

3 large potatoes, peeled and chunked bite-size
1 medium cabbage (about 2 pounds) cut into bite-size chunks (discard core and outer portions)
1 large parsnip, peeled and sliced thin
1 large turnip, peeled and sliced thin
1 large carrot, scraped and sliced thin
1 medium rutabaga, peeled and diced
1 large onion, peeled, sliced and broken into rings
1/2 stick butter, melted and divided
1/2 tsp. salt
1/4 tsp. pepper
1-1/2 cups cheddar cheese, grated or shredded

Cover the potatoes, cabbage, carrot, rutabaga, turnip and parsnip pieces with water in a sauce pan and boil, covered, until the vegetables start to soften. Using a slotted spoon, remove the cabbage after 3 minutes, all of the vegetables except the potatoes after 5 minutes and remove the potatoes after 10 minutes. Sauté the onion rings in a skillet in 1/2 of the butter. Place all of the ingredients, including the melted butter in a lightly greased baking dish or pan. Season with salt and pepper as you stir them together but save 1/2 cup of grated cheese to sprinkle on top. Bake in a pre-heated 350° oven covered, one hour.

Fish and Potato Casserole

Ingredients to serve 4:

4 fillets, about 8 oz each (Walleye works well), remove skin and bones
4 large potatoes, peeled and sliced about 1/2 inch thick
1 small onion, peeled, sliced and broken into rings
1 cup milk
2 tbsp. minced, fresh dill
4 tbsp. grated Parmesan cheese
1/2 tsp. salt
1/4 tsp. pepper
lemon pepper
Tartar sauce (optional)

In a sauce pan, cover the potato slices with water and boil (covered) 15 minutes or until they just start to soften. Drain and cool to handle. Using a lightly greased 12x12 baking dish or pan, layer the potato slices on the bottom. Pour the milk over the potatoes. Layer the onion rings on top of the potatoes. Lightly season with salt and pepper. Lay the 4 fish fillets on top of the onion rings side by side. Season with lemon pepper. Sprinkle with chopped dill. Sprinkle with Parmesan cheese (about 1 tbsp. per fillet). Bake, uncovered, in a 350° oven 20 minutes or until the fish flakes with a fork. Do not over-cook.

Wild Rice Casserole with Pheasant, Partridge, Cornish Game Hen or Duck

Ingredients:

1 game bird, well baked, seasoned with salt and pepper,
basted with soy sauce, and cut up into bite-size chunks
1 cup wild rice* , well washed
1 stick butter (1/4 pound)
2 cups diced celery
1 medium onion, chopped
1 large can mushroom pieces
1 can mushroom soup
4 tbsp. soy sauce (plus soy sauce for basting bird)

Prepare wild rice by simmering in water 30 minutes, or until well flowered. Roast bird, seasoned with salt and pepper and basted with soy sauce, until well done. Cut into bite-size pieces. In a pan, sauté the celery and onion pieces in butter. Add the meat pieces, stock from the roasting pan, drained mushrooms, mushroom soup, and 4 tbsp. soy sauce. Stir together. Place all of the above ingredients, plus the cooked wild rice, in a buttered baking dish-mix together well. Dab with butter and sprinkle a little soy sauce on top. Bake in a 350˚ oven for 20-25 minutes. Makes about 6 servings. If the birds are small, use two.

* Wild rice does not grow in Germany. This is an adoption of a German recipe by a second generation American-German family.

Ingredients to serve 2 or 3:

1 large can sauerkraut
1 can water
2 tbsp. brown sugar
8 wieners or 1/2 pound side pork or brats
2 medium potatoes, peeled and grated

Combine the sauerkraut, water and sugar and simmer over low heat 30 minutes. If you used wieners or brats, cut them into chunks and add them to the sauerkraut at the start. If you choose side pork, fry it first and add it to the kraut after it has been cooked. Add the grated potatoes, stirring them in and continue to cook another 30 minutes or until the mixture starts to thicken. Serve as is or over boiled potatoes.

Eintopfgerichte

Beef Stroganoff (German Style)

Ingredients to serve 6:

1-1/2 pounds tender beef (usually steak) cut bite-size
1 cup beef broth or consommé
1/2 pound mushrooms of your choice, sliced
1/2 cup sour cream
2 onions, sliced (broken into rings and cut into 2 inch lengths)
3 T flour, all purpose
3 T butter
salt and freshly ground pepper to taste

Roll the beef pieces in flour and brown in butter – all sides. Add onion and mushrooms while browning; stir so onion does not burn. Stir in 1 T of the flour towards the end. Add all other ingredients except sour cream and let simmer 20 minutes or until meat in tender. Stir in sour cream. Check seasoning and add more salt and/or pepper if necessary. Serve over rice or potatoes or noodles.

Desserts

Chapter Eight

Ingredients:

2 eggs
3 eggs, separated
1/2 cup butter, softened
1 cup sugar
3 squares (ounces) semi-sweet chocolate, grated
1/4 cup fine salted cracker crumbs
3/4 cup grated almonds
3/4 cup sifted flour
1 T sugar
1/2 pound fresh cherries, pitted (or maraschino)
butter and sugar for coating pan
confectioners' sugar

Pre-heat oven to 375°. Blend butter and sugar. Beat in the egg yolks and then the whole eggs. Stir in grated chocolate, cracker crumbs, flour and almonds. Beat egg whites and sugar until stiff. Combine with the above. Butter a cake pan and sprinkle with flour. Pour batter into cake pan and top with cherries. Bake 40 minutes and let cool. Remove from pan and sprinkle with confectioner's sugar.

Apple Friters *(Apfelkuchel)*

Ingredients to serve 4:
For the batter:

2 egg yolks
1 egg white, beat until stiff
1/2 cup beer
3 T sugar
2/3 cup all purpose flour
1 T butter, melted
1/2 t salt

Beat together egg yolks, beer, flour and salt. Gradually add flour until batter will stick to a spoon. Add the melted butter and let stand 30 minutes. Stir in the beaten egg white and proceed immediately to process apple slices.

Remaining ingredients:

4 large, crisp apples, cored, peeled and sliced (about two inches thick)
Cooking oil for deep fat frying
Confectioners' sugar

Just before the 30 minutes are up, begin heating the cooking oil. Dip the apple slices, one at a time, in the batter, and deep fat fry (a few slices at a time) in the hot oil. Turn slices each once so that they are a golden brown on each side. Remove with a slotted spoon and place on paper towel. Sprinkle with confectioners' sugar. Serve warm.

*Easy German Kuchen**

Ingredients:

1 loaf frozen bread dough
(thawed)
1 cup of whipping cream
1/4 cup sugar
1 T flour
1 egg

1 tsp Vanilla
2 apples, sliced
crumb topping
1/4 C butter
1/4 c sugar
1/2 c flour

Roll out dough on a floured surface as if you were making a deep dish pizza. Using a small amount of butter or margarine, grease a deep dish pizza pan. When your dough is thin enough and big enough to cover the bottom of the pan, place dough in pan. Allow dough to rise for 20 minutes. Prepare filling and crumbs while crust is rising.

Filling:
Heat cream gently (DO NOT BOIL). Use medium heat on the cooking top. In a bowl combine 1/4 cup sugar, 1 tablespoon flour and one egg. Beat until creamy. Add to warm cream and stir mixture with wire whisk until it thickens. Add 1 teaspoon of vanilla. Let mixture cool for a few minutes.

Make crumbs by cutting 1/4 cup butter into 1/4 cup sugar and 1/2 cup flour. Blend until ingredients resemble small crumbs. Set aside. Wash, peel and slice 2 apples. Spread cooled cream mixture onto dough. Spread apples evenly, top with crumbs and sprinkle with cinnamon/sugar. Bake at 375˚ for 15-20 minutes. cool slightly - cut into serving sized pieces.

* Courtesy of Joyce Pappenfus; St. Cloud MN

Strawberry-Rhubarb Dessert

Ingredients to serve 4:

1-1/2 pounds rhubarb cut into half-inch chunks
1 quart strawberries, halved or sliced
1 t vanilla
1 cup water
1 cup sugar

If rhubarb is young and fresh, just wash and cut. If older, remove stringy exterior before cutting. Place all ingredients except strawberries in a pot and simmer for ten minutes or until rhubarb is tender. Stir in strawberries and serve either hot or cold.

Sauce Made from Dried Fruit

Ingredients to serve 6:

1 pound dried fruit (dried apricots, prunes, pineapple and apple - all work well)
water - enough to cover
1 cup sugar
1 T lemon juice
lemon or orange peel as garnish

Cover fruit with water and let stand over-night. Add sugar and lemon juice and simmer 30 minutes or until fruit is soft. Serve as is, hot or cold, or pureé in a blender. Garnish with citrus peel.

Oatmeal Cookies

Ingredients for about 3 dozen cookies:

First step:

Toast one cup quick oatmeal in 2 T butter and one t sugar (in a sauce pan over low heat until brown)

Next:

Melt 1/2 stick (1/8 pound) butter and stir until well blended. Add 1/2 cup sugar and one egg and beat until well blended. Add 1/3 cup flour and 1/2 t baking powder and stir in thoroughly. Stir in 1/2 cup chopped walnuts. Bake in a pre-heated 350° oven, dropping a tablespoon of batter for each cookie onto a greased cookie sheet. Bake for about ten to twelve minutes or until brown.

Bread Pudding

Ingredients to serve 6:

6 slices stale bread (but not moldy!)
2/3 cup raisins
6 medium crisp apples, cored, peeled and sliced (thin)
1 stick butter, sliced thin (1/4 pound)
3 T sugar (divided)
2 T cinnamon
4 T flour
3 cups milk
3 eggs

Arrange 3 slices of bread on bottom of a baking dish that has been lubricated with butter. Stir together apple slices, raisins, 1 1/2 T sugar and cinnamon. Distribute over bread slices and top with remaining slices of bread. Make a batter of milk, eggs, flour and the rest of the sugar. Pour over the contents of the baking dish and dot with butter slices. Place in a pre-heated 375° oven for one hour. Serve as is or with cream (heavy or whipped)

Ingredients for about 5 dozen cookies:

4 eggs, whites only
2 T alcoholic beverage (gin, vodka, wine, etc.)
3/4 cup sugar
1/2 cup chopped walnuts or other nuts of your choosing
1 cup dates, chopped
2 T cornstarch

Beat egg whites until they start to stiffen. Add alcohol and sugar and continue to beat until stiff. Stir in dates, chopped nuts and cornstarch. Bake in a pre-heated 300° oven. Using a tablespoon, drop batter onto a greased cookie sheet. Bake twenty minutes or until cookies have turned brown.

Phleumkuchen (Plum Cake)*

Ingredients to serve 8-10:
2 cups flour
1 tsp. baking powder
3 Tbs. sugar
1/2 tsp. salt
3/4 cup butter
2 eggs
2 Tbs. cream

30 Italian Plums pitted and halved. (fresh in August and early September) Mix 2 c. flour, baking powder, salt, sugar, butter into a dough. Add 1 egg and cream. Pat into a 9" square or round pan. Fill with plums laid in rows overlapping on top of crust. Combine 1 cup sugar, 1 egg, and 2 Tbs. flour. Put mixture on top of fruit. Bake at 350° for 45 minutes to 1 hour or until solid. Best served warm.

Note: Erna used a sweet dough yeast recipe for base in a jelly roll pan also required 60 plums.
Note: Nectarines, peaches, 1 qt. of berries, such as blueberries, raspberries or cherries can be substituted. Mash berries and mix with 1 cup sugar, 1 egg, 2 Tbs. flour.

*Erna Berger's recipe; provided by Joyce Pappenfus, St. Cloud, MN.

German Rhubarb Pie*

Ingredient	Amount	Procedure
All purpose flour	2 cups	Sift together flour and salt. Use a pastry blender to cut lard into flour. Sprinkle ice cold water over dough. Gently gather dough together to form 2 balls. Chill. Roll out 1 ball of dough and use for the bottom of the pie. Rollout other ball of dough. Cut rolled dough into twelve 1/2 inch wide strips. Reserve strips to form a woven lattice for top of pie.
Salt	1 teaspoon	
Lard *(Must use Lard - DO NOT SUBSTITUTE)*	1 cup	
Ice Cold Water	4-6 tablespoons	

Ingredient	Amount	Procedure
Rhubarb, clean and diced	2 cups	Clean and dice rhubarb and set aside. Beat together the sugar, flour, egg yolks, lemon juice, and salt. Place diced rhubarb in bottom of unbaked 9 inch pie pan. Pour sugar-egg mixture over rhubarb in pie pan. Cover top of pie with woven lattice made of pie dough. allow dough to hang 1/2 inches over edge of pie pan. Trim off excess dough. Use fingers to crimp dough all around perimeter of pie. Bake at 400° for 20 minutes. Reduce temperature to 350° and bake 20 minutes longer. Remove from oven and cool on wire rack. Cut pie into 6 to 8 wedges and place each slice on a dessert plate.
Sugar	2/3 cup	
Flour	2 tablespoons	
Egg Yolks	2	
Lemon Juice	2 teaspoons	
Salt	1/8 teaspoon	

*Recipe by Barbara Pappenfus; submitted by Lynn (Pappenfus) Durrenberger.

140

German Yummy Fruit Roll*

Ingredient	Amount	Procedure
Heavy whipping cream Vanilla	1 cup 1 tablespoon	Place the 1 cup of heavy whipping cream with 1 tablespoon vanilla in a small mixing bowl and whip together until stiff. Transfer the whipped cream to a large mixing bowl.
Dates, pitted and cut Bananas, peeled and diced *(See Variation Below)* Walnut, chopped Marshmallows, miniature	1/2 pound 3 large 1 cup 1 pound	Fold the cut dates, chopped bananas, chopped walnuts, and miniature marshmallows into the whipped cream. Form mixture into a roll.
Graham Crackers, rolled fine	8 whole rectangular shape crackers or 16 square shape crackers	Coat this roll with the graham cracker crumbs. Cover with wax paper and chill in refrigerator overnight. Cut into slices. Place each slice on a dessert plate. Top with whipped cream and a maraschino cherry.

VARIATION: *Leave out Bananas and increase dates to 1 pound. This is also delicious.*

* Recipe by Hermina (Minnie) Pappenfus; submitted by Lynn (Pappenfus) Durrenberger

Desserts

German Dutch Cream Cake*

Ingredient	Amount	Procedure
Granulated Sugar	1-1/4 cup	Place sugar, lard, salt and vanilla in large mixing bowl. Cream well
Lard or Shortening	1/2 cup	
Salt	3/4 teaspoon	
Vanilla	1 teaspoon	
Eggs	2	Add eggs one at a time, beating well after each addition.
Cocoa Powder	1/4 cup	Add cocoa and blend well.
All purpose flour, sifted	1-3/4 cup	Sift together flour, baking powder and baking soda. Add flour to creamed mixture, alternately with evaporated milk, beginning and ending with the flour. Mix well between each addition. Pour batter into two 8 inch round greased and floured cake pans. Bake 350° for 25-30 minutes. Remove from oven, cool. Cut each layer into 2 layers to yield 4 layers total.
Baking Powder	1 teaspoon	
Baking Soda	1/4 teaspoon	
Evaporated milk, undiluted	1 cup	
Heavy whipping cream	1-1/2 cups	Combine these three ingredients and whip until stiff. Use between layers and on top of 4th layer. Refrigerate cake 2-3 hours.
Vanilla	1 teaspoon	
Powdered sugar	4 tablespoons	

* Recipe by Alice Altstatt; submitted by Lynn (Pappenfus) Durrenberger.

German Chocolate Spice Cake*

Ingredient	Amount	Procedure
Granulated Sugar	1 cup	Place sugar, lard (or shortening), cloves, cinnamon, allspice and 1/2 teaspoon Cloves, ground cocoa powder in large mixing bowl. Cream well until all ingredients are well mixed.
Lard or shortening	1/2 cup	
Cinnamon, ground	1 teaspoon	
Allspice	1 teaspoon	
Cocoa Powder	2 tablespoons	
Eggs	1	Add egg and beat well.
All purpose flour, sifted	1-1/2 cups	Sift flour with baking soda. Add flour to creamed mixture alternately with buttermilk, beginning and ending with the flour. Mix well with each addition. Pour batter into two 8 inch round greased and floured cake pans. Bake 350˚ for 25-30 minutes. Remove from oven, cool. Frost layers, top and sides with Chocolate Fudge Icing. (below)
Baking Soda	1 teaspoon	
Buttermilk	1 cup	
Butter	1/2 cup	Melt together butter and cocoa powder. Place sifted powdered sugar and salt in large mixing bowl. Scald milk by heating it over medium temperature until milk comes to rolling boil. Watch carefully so it does not boil over. Pour scalded milk over powdered sugar and stir until dissolved. Beat in vanilla and melted butter-chocolate mixture. Continue beating until thick enough to spread. Frost layers, top and sides.
Cocoa Powder	3/4 cup	
Powdered Sugar, sifted	4 cups	
Salt	1 teaspoon	
Milk, scalded	2/3 cup	
Vanilla		

* Recipe by Alice Altstatt; submitted by Lynn (Pappenfus) Durrenberger.

German Old Fashioned Cranberry Sauce*

Ingredient	Amount	Procedure
Raw Cranberries- *(You may use fresh or frozen)*	1 pound	Cut the cored and seeded apples and oranges into quarters or eighths. Run the cranberries and small pieces of apples and oranges through a hand food grinder. Instead of the hand grinder you may use an electric food processor with a chopper attachment. Place the ground cranberries, apples and oranges in a large saucepan.
Red apples with seeds and inner core removed.	2 large	
Orange with the seeds and inner core removed. Also cut off blossom end and bottom end.	1 large	
Sugar	2 cups	Add the sugar and water to the saucepan containing the ground cranberries, apples and oranges.
Water	1 cup	
		Cook over low heat only until mixture is thickened, and bright, clear red. Do not over-cook. Over cooking will make it very dark and bitter. Place in a large glass bowl. Serve with roast turkey, chicken or duck.

* Recipe by Alice Altstatt; submitted by Lynn (Pappenfus) Durrenberger.

German Ginger Crinkle Cookies*

Ingredient	Amount	Procedure
Lard or shortening	1-1/2 cups	Cream together lard (shortening)
Granulated sugar	2 cups	sugar, eggs, molasses, ginger
Eggs, large	2	cloves, cinnamon, salt, and
Molasses	1/2 cup	baking soda.
Ginger	2 tsps.	
Cloves	2 tsps.	
Cinnamon	2 tsps.	
Salt	1 tsp.	
Baking Soda	1 T plus 1 tsp.	
All purpose flour, sifted	4 cups	Gradually stir in flour and mix well. Chill
Additional	Enough in which	dough. Form dough into 48 balls. Roll
granulated sugar	to roll balls	each ball in granulated sugar. Evenly
		space sugar coated balls of dough onto
		lightly greased cookie sheet. Flatten each
		ball slightly with palm of your hand.
		Bake at 350° for about 10-15 minutes
		OR until light brown. Watch closely so
		cookies do not burn. Cookies will flatten
		and crinkle while baking.
		Yield – 4 dozen

* Recipe by Alice Altstatt; submitted by Lynn (Pappenfus) Durrenberger

German Filled Cookies*

Ingredient	Amount	Procedure
Dates (or raisins)	1 cup	Combine dates (or raisins), grated rind and sugar in large saucepan.
Grated lemon or orange rind	2 teaspoons	
Granulated sugar	1 cup	
All purpose flour	1 tablespoon	Mix flour with 1/2 cup water and add to dates (or raisins). Cook over low heat until mixture in thick. Stir occasionally to prevent burning. Cool date (or raisin) mixture thoroughly and use as filling for the tiny pies.
Water	1/2 cup	

Ingredient	Amount	Procedure
Sugar	1 cup	Cream sugar, lard (or shortening), salt and vanilla well.
Lard or shortening	1 cup	
Salt	1 teaspoon	
Vanilla	1 teaspoon	
Egg	1	Add egg and beat well.

Baking soda	1 teaspoon	Mix baking soda with flour.
Flour, sifted	3 cups	
Sour Cream	1 cup	Add flour-baking soda mixture alternately with sour cream, beginning and ending with flour mixture. Chill dough for 4 hours. Roll out dough to 1/8 inch thick. Cut out circles of dough using a 2-1/2 inch round cookie cutter. Place cut circles of dough on lightly greased cookie sheet. Top each circle of dough with 1 tablespoon filling. Cover with another circle of dough. Using a fork, press edges of tiny pie together. Using a knife, vent each pie by cutting top with 3 slashes.

Bake at 350° for about 8 minutes until light brown.

Yield – about 3 dozen cookies

* Recipe by Hermina (Minnie) Pappenfus; submitted by Lynn (Pappenfus) Durrenberger.

German Chokecherry Jelly*

Ingredient	Amount	Procedure
Chokecherries, raw, cleaned with stems and leaves removed	10 cups or 3-1/2 pounds	Place cleaned chokecherries and apple pieces in large stainless steel pot. Add just enough water to barely cover berries and apple pieces. Bring to a boil and simmer with lid on pot for 30 minutes. Arrange 2 layers of cheesecloth in a colander that is set in a large stainless steel pot. Pour cooked fruit and juice into colander containing cheesecloth. Collect juice into the pot. Discard cooked fruit solids. Measure 3-1/2 cups juice. Use this to make jelly.
Apples, raw, cut in eighths	2	
Jelly jars	6	Before you start cooking juice with SURE JELL, you must start sterilizing jars, lids, rings by doing the following: Place jars, rings and lids in large pot and set pot on burner on stove. Fill pot and jars with water. Bring to a boil and keep on medium boil until ready to fill with jells. (see below)
Lids	6	
Rings	6	
Cooked, strained chokecherry juice	3-1/2 cups	While jars, lids and rings are being sterilized (see above) do the following: Place juice In large stainless steel pot. Add SURE JELL and stir until dissolved. Bring to boil and boil for one minute while stirring constantly.
SURE JELL	1 package	
Granulated cane sugar	4-1/2 cups	

Add sugar and stir until dissolved. Bring to a boil and boil for one minute while stirring constantly. To set up work area for fast efficient production in filling the jars with jelly do the following: Place cake pan on 2 trivets situated on counter. To left of cake pan place stainless steel bowl. Quickly transfer pot of boiling jelly to cake pan. Place jelly jar inside bowl, immediately ladle boiling jelly into jar, add lid and ring, screw tightly. Invert filled hot jars onto folded terry towel placed on counter. TO PREVENT BURNING YOUR HANDS WHILE HANDLING SCALDING HOT JARS, LIDS, AND RINGS, WEAR HOT PAD HOLDER STYLE GLOVES. Repeat above process to fill other 5 jars with jelly. Leave jars inverted for 1 hour, then place in upright position and leave for 24 hours to cool Store in cupboard away from heat at room temperature.

YIELD: 6 EIGHT OUNCE JARS OF JELLY

* Recipe by Ardelle Wilkes; submitted by Lynn (Pappenfus) Durrenberger.

Home Brew
Chapter Nine

German Dandelion Wine*

Ingredient	Amount	Procedure
Dandelion Blossoms	2 quarts	Clean the dandelion blossoms thoroughly by hand but do not wash.
Water	Enough water to cover 2 quarts blossoms	Put blossoms in large kettle with just enough water to cover blossoms and simmer slowly until they come to a boil. Let mixture stand for 24 hours. Strain blossoms and discard them but reserve the strained blossom juice for the wine.
Orange Juice Lemon Juice	From 2 large oranges From 2 large lemons	Add orange juice and lemon juice to the large kettle containing the strained blossom juice and mix well. Pour the juice mixture into a gallon jug and set aside.
Granulated Sugar Water	3 pounds 1 gallon	In a separate kettle dissolve 3 pounds of granulated sugar in 1 gallon of water and simmer over low heat until it comes to a boil. Add enough of this boiled sugar water mixture to the jug containing the juice so the juice completely fills the gallon jug. Cover top of jug with a clean cloth. Keep the jug filled daily with the reserved sugar water mixture. Each day skim off the heavy sediment that rises to the top. Do this until the dandelion wine stops working, then cork it. Enjoy.

* Recipe by Hermina (Minnie) Pappenfus; submitted by Lynn (Pappenfus) Durrenberger.

German Beer *

Measure 3 quarts of water into a large kettle. Meanwhile, remove the label from a can of malt; open the can and set the can in hot water for five minutes.

Bring the kettle of water to a boil. Empty the malt into the boiling water and stir.

Add 5-1/4 cups of sugar. The mixture will foam at first. Remove the kettle from the heat before the foam reaches the top of the kettle and spills over. When the foam subsides, return the kettle to the heat and let the mixture boil for ten minutes.

Meanwhile, put 4-1/4 gallons of cold water into a crock (if using hard water, 1 tsp. pickling salt must be added). Allow the malt mixture to cool and add to the crock. When it has cooled to between 65° and 75°, sprinkle with yeast.

Cover crock with a clean cloth or plastic sheet and let ferment until specific gravity reaches 1.003 to 1.009

Siphon wort into a clean container. Stir 1 cup of sugar into 1 cup of warm water and then add and stir this into the mixture (for priming). Let stand one day. It is now ready to bottle and cap.

Let bottled beer stand 7 days at room temperature to condition, then store for 3 to 4 weeks in a cool place. Now enjoy! (Alcoholic content will test 5.9 percent.)

Important! All equipment used should be sterilized. One T Hilex to one gallon of water works well. Then rinse with water. This is necessary to remove any bacteria which might effect the taste of the finished product.

* Recipe by Paul Weber; submitted by Greg Liefermann, Staples.

Beer Recipe #2

For 5 gallons — One 3 pound can Hop Flavored Malt Syrup — 3 pounds granulated sugar — one cake compressed or dehydrated yeast. Dissolve syrup and sugar in boiling hot water — pour into cold water to make five gallons — allow to further cool for two hours, then add one cake yeast. Cover crock or other fermenting vessel with clean cloth. Keep in a cool, dark place. Watch carefully and when bubbles of gas cease coming to surface, fermentation has been completed and the liquid should be quite clear. (approximately four days).

Now siphon or pour off clear liquid to another clean crock, leaving the thick sediment behind. To the liquid in the second crock add 1/4 pound granulated sugar and stir until dissolved. Fill into bottles by siphoning or pouring. Cap and immediately store in a cool dark place. The beverage will be ready for use when clear — requires one to two weeks.

One crock can be eliminated if the liquid is siphoned directly into the bottles from the fermenting crock. In this case, place 1/2 teaspoon sugar in each pint or one teaspoon in each quart bottle. Best consistent results can be obtained if a five gallon bottle is used instead of a crock for the fermenting vessel, using a water seal. All vessels and tubing should be entirely clean and sanitary before use. A 2-3% warm lye solution is an excellent one for this purpose. Rinse with water after the use of lye solution.

Creator unknown; submitted by Greg Liefermann, Staples, MN.